THE WORLD'S GREAT
Luxury Fishing Resorts

Wits End Guest Ranch

*In-depth profiles featuring twenty
world-class fishing destinations*

**MICHAEL CALDWELL
LIFESTYLE PUBLISHING GROUP**

THE WORLD'S GREAT
Luxury Fishing Resorts

ISBN: 0-9692129-4-1

Cover & Book Design: Bill Engelhart, Florida Imaging

Front Cover Photograph: Sonora Resort

Back Cover Photograph: Spotted Horse Ranch

Printed in Hong Kong by Elegance Printing & Book Binding Company
through www.booksjustbooks.com

*A special thanks to the talented people at Florida Imaging
for taking creative layout to the next level.*

Spotted Horse Ranch

TABLE OF CONTENTS

Ruby Springs Lodge

At the end of my travels, I had discovered a profound truth — what I now think of as the essence of fishing. It is not simply the luxuries inherent in the sport — fresh air, rivers, oceans, lakes, wilderness, and the thrill of the hunt — it is the ultimate form of natural meditation.

INTRODUCTION

This book was borne from a love of three of life's great pleasures — good fishing, fine food, and deluxe lodging. There is only one place where you can enjoy all of these experiences at the same time. That place is a luxury fishing resort. Whether they call themselves a resort, a lodge, a ranch or a club, these fishing destinations all have the three ingredients necessary for those who choose to take a fishing vacation in style and comfort. Although the central theme is fishing, it is as much about the luxurious lodgings, gourmet food and spectacular settings that come with it.

Research for the book involved hours of travel through the electronic ether and months of travel through the United States and Canada. My journey by land, sea and air tallied 12,000 miles, 200 miles and 8,000 miles respectively. It was, without question, the most exciting, enlightening and enjoyable time of my life. The people I met — resort owners, fishing guides, chefs and guests; and the places I traveled — Alaska, the Rocky Mountain states and the Canadian wilderness, were incomparable to any life experience.

The twenty fishing destinations profiled in this book offer, in my opinion, the best possible experience for the vacationing fisherman. Common to all are deluxe accommodations, professional staff, top quality equipment and creative cuisine. And of course, access to an exceptional natural resource that virtually guarantees a great fishing adventure.

Although the book is presented in a coffee table format, it is designed to be much more than a plethora of pretty pictures. It is loaded with prose. It was written in the first person simply because I wanted to offer the reader a glimpse into the window of my actual journey.

Topics discussed in each chapter are consistent throughout the book. Subjects deemed of interest to the reader include the place, the people, the fishing, the facilities, the cuisine and guest comments. For those places that also offer key activities other than angling, they are detailed under the subject called leisure pursuits. There is also a section titled, *"A Day in The Life Of…"* Here, I have documented the activities of one of the guests from sunrise through sunset.

At the end of my travels, I had discovered a profound truth — what I now think of as the essence of fishing. It is not simply the luxuries inherent in the sport — fresh air, rivers, oceans, lakes, wilderness, and the thrill of the hunt. It is the ultimate form of natural meditation. The true fisherman, when out for a day on the water, will become completely focused on his quest. As he does so, the anxieties of everyday living will quietly disappear…leaving a sense of tranquility unlike any other he will find. And to achieve this state of mind while sitting in the lap of luxury is, to me, the best of all worlds.

BARANOF WILDERNESS LODGE

the place

This is Russian Alaska — a land explored by merchants of the Czar. They came for whales and fur. And while whey never settled, they left the residue of their culture. Witness the name of the island — Baranof, the name of the closest town — Sitka.

It is a rugged realm, wrought with cascading waterfalls, jagged peaks, giant glaciers and mountain passes. Baranof Wilderness Lodge sits on the eastern side of Baranof Island, on the inside passage. On the shores of the Warm Springs Bay you'll find this unique fishing resort. This bay was named for the warm mineral springs that, beginning centuries ago, have been enjoyed by the Tlingit Indians, then the Russians, and now guests of the lodge.

The lodge itself was originally built in the 1980's by the grandson of Alaska's most beloved territorial governor, Ernest "Pop" Gruening. Since then, it has been named by the prestigious Best Places Alaska as the "Very Best in the Region" and has earned a four-star rating.

Another far-flung hideaway accessible only by boat or floatplane, the flight in from Sitka is almost worth the price of admission. As you fly over spectacular waterfalls and glaciers, through mountain passes, and over a roaring river, remember that the best is yet to come. Dozens of bays, estuaries, fishing streams and lakes are within a short boat ride or hike from the lodge. And because this is the richest spawning ground for salmon in the world, you are probably here to angle.

Electricity is provided via the lodge's own hydroelectric plant on Sadie Creek, one of many mountain streams that wind through the lush, ancient forests surrounding the lodge. The fact that they make twenty-four-hour electricity a feature underscores how remote this lodge really is. But, as is generally the rule, the more remote a place is, the richer the wildlife experience.

It is immediately apparent why they call this place a "wilderness" lodge. Before I had even settled in to my cabin, we saw a brown bear and then spotted, and even heard, a humpback whale.

the people

Baranof Wilderness Lodge is owned and managed by Mike Trotter, a veteran of the Alaskan wilderness for more than two decades. Red haired, red bearded, and the picture of what you would expect an Alaskan outdoorsman to look like, he is keen about everything - from the current fishing hot-spots to the latest California wine selections.

Their crew of guides are all great fly fishing instructors. And for three weeks each year they bring in the "top gun" — celebrity guide, instructor and light tackle specialist Ken Hanley. He is regarded by many to be one of the most knowledgeable and experienced inshore fly fishermen in the world. His expertise is equaled only by his ability to communicate inside information to his students. This place is unique in their ability to offer guests a salt water light tackle fly fishing program. Also worthy of note is their annual one-week Wildlife Photography seminar. It is hosted by renowned naturalist and photographer John Hendrickson, whose photos you'll see in this chapter.

The lodge is staffed by people who might be more passionate about the outdoors than anyone I've ever met. They work hard and continuously to minimize the impact of man on this pristine area. While doing this, they also take great pride in making your vacation a classy yet casual experience. I quickly came to realize that most of them work here because of their love of fishing and the Alaskan wilderness living.

the fishing

From the Baranof Lodge, you have access to countless fishing holes as well as all five species of Pacific salmon. They catch kings up to fifty pounds, chum from nine to seventeen pounds, along with sockeye, pinks and silver salmon. Transportation to the fishing holes is provided by the lodge's fleet of twenty-four-foot cabin cruisers, and they limit each boat to four guests. They also have a smaller fleet of mobile skiffs and runabouts to facilitate their fresh and salt water light tackle and fly fishing.

If you feel like going deep, mammoth halibut lurk in the depths. The halibut in this area of the world are leviathans. The lodge record is 380 pounds. And even without being asked, I found myself looking at more than a few pictures of man-sized halibut caught by their guests. While they practice catch-and-release in all freshwater fisheries, the lodge will prepare one box of salmon or halibut for you to take home.

Late on the afternoon of my visit, three of the guests came in from their day on the water. They had all joined the Century Club — all caught halibut weighing over 100 pounds. Here's the amazing part. They caught the three fish, weighing in at 187, 142 and 106 pounds, at the same moment in time. The ultimate triple-header.

For guests who enjoy fly fishing and light tackle adventure, there are a large variety of experiences available here. The local waters are world class venues for saltwater salmon and shallow-water rockfish. These game fish are a perfect match for intimate encounters on ultralight gear. Whether you are drifting near kelp forests, wading estuary flats or working along a rocky shoreline, it won't be long until you're hooked into one of these feisty fighters. For the more adventuresome souls, whose thirst for

outdoor adventure is not quite quenched by the Wilderness Lodge alone, Mike Trotter also owns Beyond Boundaries Expeditions. Among other things, they operate, under a special permit from the Tongass National Forest, a Base Camp Safari. From Sitka, you are flown to their camp at Kelp Bay. They "rough it" here with spacious cabin tents, comfortable bunks, hot showers and hearty home-cooked meals. The incredible stream fishing is very popular, and Mike provides a boat and guide for every two guests.

the facilities

The accommodations here are in the form of private lodging, all elegantly furnished, spacious and comfortable. They have deluxe appointments, like handcrafted leather-on-wood rocking chairs; and some have fireplaces. Although each cabin is unique, they all have one thing in common - a waterfront view. Considering the wilderness that you're sitting in, it is a special treat to awaken every morning to hot coffee that's been delivered to your cabin porch. And from this porch, with a little luck, you can catch a glimpse of the whales the Russians sought a century ago.

After a hard day's fishing, some guests like to relax in the nearby hot springs, just like the Tlingit and Russian explorers who preceded them. The lodge also features two hot tubs. A redwood tub situated in a grove of trees overlooking a nearby mountain stream, or the tub on the deck, offering a magnificent panorama of the bay, mountains and wildlife.

Cabin cruisers take you to remote venues for fishing or sightseeing. Kayaks and outboard-powered skiffs are available to explore the protected waters of the bay, and boats and canoes are strategically placed on nearby lakes.

the cuisine

Even in this remote outpost, Mike Trotter and company pride themselves on serving a more civilized fare. In fact, the menu reads like it was lifted from a gourmet bistro in a trendy upscale urban setting. All meals are perfectly accented with vegetables and herbs grown right here in the their own gardens. Many nights you'll feast on seafood and vegetables harvested literally hours before. And, of course, all meals are served with home-baked Baranof Bread.

The purveyors of the Baranof Wilderness Lodge are exceptionally proud of their extensive wine list. And so they should be. All wines are hand-picked from the Sonoma and Napa Valleys in California for just the right complement to every meal.

The evening I was there they served dinner buffet style. Your choices were incredible. Arrayed on the table in front of us was: fresh halibut encrusted with almonds in lemon butter sauce; grilled salmon with green peppercorn cream sauce; fresh crab steamed and served au natural; and pork loin roulade stuffed with house smoked apple, onions and spicy sausage. Side dishes included a black bean and rice pilaf, fresh vegetable medley and home baked breads.

a day in the life of...the good 'ol boys

The day I checked in, there were eleven guests, all from the state of Texas. Three of these guys have been here in preceding years — Wayne Cecil, David "Chigger" King and Damon "Big Country" Ward. This time they brought some friends. As a group, they get up around 6:30am for some fresh coffee and juice. Then it's down for breakfast at 7:00 o'clock. They all get down to the dock, meet up with their guides for the day, and start fishing by 7:30 am. Lunch is served on the boat, or shore lunch along the river bank, allowing maximum fishing time.

Everyone arrives back at the lodge by 5:00 pm. For the next hour, they show their catches and discuss their highlights of the day. Up to the cabins for a shower and change, then all meet for drinks on the deck of the lodge. Dinner is served between 6:30 pm and 7:00 pm. One of the Texans told me the food was so good that "it'll make your tongue want to slap your brain." He was right. Afterwards, the "fun board" comes out, and Mike walks you through the options for the coming day. Each guest chooses their next activity and records it on the board.

guest comments

"I wanted to write to express our gratitude for the very special and memorable week we spent at Baranof Wilderness Lodge. Your unbridled enthusiasm and obvious love of the wilderness, fishing and your marvelous staff sets the tone for the wonderful spirit of the lodge. We feel very fortunate to have had the opportunity to experience your beautiful little spot on the globe."

— *Jane & Kameron Maxwell*

"Absolutely, without a doubt the best vacation we have ever had. Each and everyone of you and your staff was terrific; every meal a gourmet feast, the whales, eagles, bears, salmon, halibut and the most incredible scenery. We are coming back."

— *Paul & Susan Feinberg*

"Dear Grandpa:

Thank you for taking me to Alaska. I had so much fun. I bet I will remember this trip for the rest of my life. All of us caught more fish than we will ever catch in our lives. This was a very cool experience for Talbot and me."

— *Ryan Sanderson*

directions

Their lodge is located on the east side of Baranof Island, twenty air miles from Sitka. Most visitors fly into Ketchikan, then continue on to Sitka. From there they can get to the lodge either on a short, spectacular flight by seaplane, or on a more leisurely-paced ferry boat ride from Sitka to Warm Springs Bay. For more information visit their website at — www.flyfishalaska.com.

BUFFALO CREEK RANCH

the place

A list of the trappers and early explorers who have passed through this area reads like a "Who's Who of the American West." Joseph Bijeau was one of the first in 1820, but the likes of Kit Carson, Jim Bridger, and John C. Fremont are among the many others.

Just 120 miles from Denver in northwest Colorado, in the valley first named New Park, then later North Park, sits the Buffalo Creek Ranch. It lies in a spectacular circular valley, walled in on all sides by snow-capped mountains whose spring thaws are the beginnings of the great North Platte River. As John Fremont described, "no river could ask for a more beautiful origin."

Mining and prospecting lured the first permanent settlers in the 1870's, but when the silver and gold diminished, lush meadows fed by plentiful streams, and abundant game led the way to North Park's ranching history. Long winters have kept many settlers out, which has turned out to be a good thing. The area is still untamed, sparsely populated and burgeoning with wildlife.

The plethora and variety of streams and lakes provide fly fishermen the unique opportunity to score a "Rocky Mountain Grand Slam" during their visit by catching one each of the area's trout species: the rainbow, brook, brown and cutthroat.

The unparalleled beauty and seclusion of this resort is the perfect getaway for the naturalist and photographer, as well as the fly fishing afficionado. Resident elk, along with mule deer, moose, antelope, eagle, hawks and eagles, coyotes, waterfowl and various other birds are common sights in and around their property. More elusive, but thrilling, is the chance to spot a bobcat, mountain lion or black bear.

The Buffalo Creek Ranch is a working ranch. Guests can witness the history and tradition each day as professional cowboys work the ranch much as it was done back in the nineteenth century. Despite its nineteenth-century character, this resort features twenty-first century amenities, including a recently built three-story lodge.

the people

It is ironic that the resort with the highest acreage is owned by a man who insists on keeping the lowest profile. Dick, a recently retired, successful businessman and avid sportsman his entire life, had owned a nearby ranch for ten years prior to the Buffalo Creek coming up for sale. He bought the ranch simply because the property was so unique — spectacular and diverse scenery, seclusion and superb fishing and hunting. The ranch is managed by a husband-and-wife team, John and Mical, and meticulously cared for by a dedicated staff of four other families that live on the property.

Dick believes that nobody ever really owns the land; we are just temporary tenants and stewards in charge of preserving it. Western ranches are continually being subdivided and developed, destroying the ranching heritage and critical wildlife habitat. His desire to prevent this becomes obvious during your first visit. There is a strong sense that nothing much has changed here over the last century. And they plan on keeping it that way.

The ranch staff is committed to providing you with a world-class vacation experience. They know the water you're fishing, the trails you're riding and the land you are hunting.

the fishing

This is Western fly fishing like people have read about in books or seen in movies. Buffalo Creek Ranch has access to more than ten miles of private streams, each possessing a little different character. Deep undercut banks, beaver ponds, deep holes and inspiring riffles and runs provide more angling opportunities than you could cover in a solid week of fishing.

These streams are rich in aquatic insects. Dry fly fishermen can expect hatches of callibaetis, pale morning duns, tricos and caddis in the mornings, evenings and overcast days. During midday, when the trout aren't rising, attractor patterns such as large stimulaters, trudes and grasshoppers can produce unbelievable strikes. Standard nymph imitations provide many hook-ups when top water action slows down.

There are also five private lakes on the ranch, each carefully managed to offer a variety of trophy trout. Both trout and insects thrive in these fertile lakes producing excellent hatches, with superb dry fly fishing, and healthy fish whose acrobatics are sure to test your leader's strength.

Buffalo Creek is a full-service resort, providing for all the extras a fisherman may need; transportation to and from the fishing holes, the best local guides, lessons for beginners and Orvis equipment. They also have

the Li'l Buffalo Fly Shop on premises. You can purchase favorite local flies and gear, try your hand at tying flies, or just relax and listen to Buffalo Creek flowing by.

Stream fishing is generally available from mid-June through mid-September. The lake fishing starts a month earlier, spanning from mid-May through September. From this point on, they reserve the ranch for big game hunters.

the facilities

This resort is unique to all others in three ways. It is the newest, taking guests only since 2001. It is the largest, encompassing more than 14,000 private acres. And despite its vastness, they have opted to cater to the fewest number of guests at any one time. A couple can often have the ranch to themselves, and

management likes to keep the maximum number at four, unless there is a reservation for a group. The reason for the low guest count is the conscious decision of the proprietors to minimally impact this natural setting. It also ensures that you will receive personal attention and fully experience the solitude the ranch affords.

Upon my arrival, I met up with John and immediately asked him to show me around the place. He asked what part? Well, all of it. He grinned and told me that would be fine. Six hours later we were back at the lodge. The scope and diversity of their property defies belief. From mountains of pine and aspen, to meadows with meandering streams, to rolling plains of sagebrush, we covered it all. Along the way, near the lakes, rivers and streams, we saw elk, antelope, mule deer, horses and even a hawk overhead. You could easily spend half your vacation just exploring the vast and varied landscape.

In the center of this property sits the lodge. It is an entirely modern structure, built in 1999. Featured are six bedrooms with three contemporary bathrooms. Beds range from queen size to side-by-side twins in one of the rooms. There are two fully-stocked kitchens, one where meals are provided and the other available if you desire a midday or late night snack.

Inside each room is a tremendous blend of the old and new. Decor that conjures up memories of the past — glass-fronted wood stoves and cathedral ceiling windows offering views of the surrounding ranch, plus deep comfortable sofas, books and satellite television. They even have a hot tub built outside, only a few steps from your door. For guests who desire to ride the high country, horses awaiting a saddle are as close as the barn. Their experienced wranglers will match riders with the right horses.

For those looking to sharpen their shooting skills, Buffalo Creek has a professional trap range for the shotgun, and a 100-yard rifle range for the rifle enthusiast. This is used both for practice and the "sighting-in" of your rifle.

leisure pursuits

During the summer months, guests that need a diversion from all the fishing, can take a trail ride on one of their horses enjoying the scenery, wildlife and magnificent views of the Continental Divide. Real cowboys do real work here, and folks who demonstrate their ability on horseback are welcome to pitch in on a cattle drive, if one is occurring during their visit.

For guests who like to hunt elk and deer, the ranch offers some of the best big game hunting in Colorado. Their valley is private and exclusive. It provides a natural harbor to the large resident herd as well as those migrating throughout the fall each year.

Buffalo Lake, popular among fishermen, is also equipped with a kayak, sailboat, drift boat and canoes as a means to enjoy the wonderful views, including the elk who come down for a game of water tag. Many guests enjoy hiking and photographing the natural beauty of this ranch. They also have limited openings in the winter where guests can enjoy the ranch on cross-country skis or snowshoes. Many also take advantage of "feeding" with the cowboys — riding along on the horse-drawn sleigh used to feed the cattle in times of deep snow.

Although very secluded, Buffalo Creek Ranch is close to many areas offering much in the way of leisure activities. At different times throughout the year, there is white-water rafting, downhill skiing, hot air ballooning, rodeos and a variety of art galleries in nearby Steamboat Springs. The ranch also lies close to Rocky Mountain National Park, the Arapaho National Wildlife Refuge and numerous designated Wilderness Areas.

the cuisine

The hearty and delicious meals here are served family style. Tables overlook the deck, the hot tub and the surrounding mountains. They offer a variety of menu options and allow you to select from them in your pre-trip planning. A nice touch. Streamside or lakeside lunches are also available so you can enjoy a peaceful picnic and fisherman won't lose valuable time when the hatch is on.

On the first evening of my visit, we sat down to dinner at 6:30 pm. The main course featured their version of "surf and turf" — barbecued steak and salmon filets served with mashed potatoes topped with diced bacon and chives, a selection of vegetables and a delicious coleslaw. After drawing a breath, dessert appeared. A homemade cheesecake topped with fresh raspberries.

guests comments

"We loved every minute up here. It's so peaceful, much open space. Certainly the best kept ranch we've seen with so much that you can learn from what it takes to run cattle, to riding horses on a ridge line, to shooting trap. The wildlife is amazing too. It was really spectacular to see the elk and hear the bugling at dusk. Lastly the fishing was great! Even in this low water year…the biggest trout we've ever hooked. We'll be back for sure."

— *Rob Park, Marblehead, Massachusetts*

"Buffalo Creek Ranch is a great fly-fishing retreat. We caught well over 100 large fish in just one day! The lodge was secluded and comfortable, the food excellent, and the personal attention to our needs was balanced with a respect for our privacy. I would highly recommend it."

— *David Manross, Denver, Colorado*

"This is a wonderful operation. I cannot thank Dick enough for opening up this beautiful ranch to allow us lucky folks to visit paradise. John runs a great operation. he has done a wonderful job managing the wildlife on the ranch…it is so beautiful here, can't wait to come back."

— *Timothy O'Neill, Frankfort, New York*

directions

Most visitors will fly into Denver International Airport, and then take a two-and-a-half hour drive to arrive at the ranch. From the airport, get onto I-70 heading west out of Denver. Take the Empire/Winter Park exit onto Hwy. 40 west. Stay on 40 through to Granby. About 3 miles west of Granby (and after going over the Colorado River), take the first right on 125 North toward Walden/Rand. Stay on this road through Rand. Four miles past, take the first left on County Road 28. Go one mile, then turn left on CR 28A. This road ends under the ranch sign. Continue on the driveway until a fork in the road (1.5 mi) and turn left. Follow the road for another 1/2 mile and go right at first fork. The lodge entrance is your first left under the wooden arch. For information visit their website at — www.buffalocreek-ranch.com.

AL CAUCCI'S
DELAWARE RIVER CLUB

the place

Located on the West Branch of the Delaware River in northern Pennsylvania, the Delaware River Club is just a mile upstream from Hancock, New York, on the Pennsylvania side of the river. The West Branch is the most renowned trout river east of the Rocky Mountains, and has been named by *Sports Afield* magazine as the second best trout river in the entire country. *Fly Fisherman* magazine called the West Branch the "Big Horn of the East."

Part of the lure of this fly-fishing resort is its proximity to the population centers on the east coast. It's only 2¹/₂ hours from downtown New York City, three hours from Philadelphia, and just over four hours from Boston and Washington, D.C. For the busy executive looking to get away for a weekend, this proximity beats a cross-country flight hands down.

My visit to this resort took place during the first week of May. Upon my arrival I was greeted by several staff members, including General Manager Jeff White. We had just sat down in the living room to get acquainted when the host, Al Caucci, showed up. He wanted to show me the "place." Little did I know this would take the better part of an hour, and involve the use of his four-wheel drive to cover an expanse of more than 500 acres.

It is called the Delaware River *Club* for a reason. It has been designed much like a private country club, and includes the lodge, deluxe guest rooms, and beautiful log homes in a planned community with homesites that are available at the club.

The Delaware River Club has everything the fly fisherman needs, including schools, guide service, fly shop, complete hatch information and lots of private river access. They also provide facilities for the whole family. When not fishing, guests can swim, use the hiking trails, practice in the trout pond, or just kick back on a porch overlooking the river.

the people

The fishing lodge is unique. What sets it apart from all others is not the place — it's the person. While guests enjoy all the style and comfort associated with a great lodge, the main draw is the owner and fly fisherman extraordinaire Al Caucci. He has compiled more than four decades of fly fishing experience and shares his wisdom in the form of the Al Caucci Fly-fishing Schools since 1984, as well as "bonefish schools" in the Bahamas and other hosted trips around the world.

Since writing his first book, Hatches, some twenty years ago, Al has become something of a "cult" figure for the expert technical fisherman in the unique world of fly fishing. Caucci has authored a total of five books on fly fishing, including the definitive work on the subject, Hatches II. This book was recently hailed by *Field & Stream* magazine as one of the "25 best fishing books in print" and by *Trout* magazine as one of the most important books in the last thirty years.

The fly fishing school offered here will save a novice angler at least five years of learning on their own. The basic course will prepare the beginner to fly fish by the time they leave the resort. It is a complete on-the-stream fly-fishing course, not simply casting lessons.

There is also the Advance River Guided Program, always taught by Al Caucci and his select staff. This class is for the intermediate to expert fisherman who wants to improve upon their already well-developed skills.

the fishing

The Delaware River, as fishing goes, was until recently a very well kept secret. The West Branch, East Branch (including Beaverkill) and Mainstream combine to offer one of the largest trout systems in the country. The West Branch and Mainstream of this river are the home of a unique strain of wild rainbow and brown trout. These trout are widely considered to be some of the "hottest" fish in the world. And a fish survey done several years back revealed an astonishing fact - the trout in this river average an impressive fifteen to sixteen inches. Even catching a  twenty-inch fish seldom raises an eyebrow around here. On the day I arrived, Jeff White landed a twenty-six inch wild brown right out in front of the lodge in an area called the "home pool."

The well-equipped fly shop aids guests immensely in their quest for the ultimate fishing experience. The shop contains all the fly patterns necessary to fish the Delaware hatches, and most other hatches across the country. Caucci and Nastasi have designed a line of flies called "Compara-flies' that have proven to be lethal on the elusive wild trout. Al's "comparadun" is now one of the most famous trout flies in the world. It can be found in just about any fly shop and catalog in the country, and was recently included in *Field & Stream's* "Deadly dozen."

Guests are outfitted to cover the more than thirty superhatches, including every local species in every phase of emergence — nymph, emerger, dun and spinner. Wherever mayflies, caddis and stoneflies exist, be it on the Delaware or not, fly fishermen can use these patterns.

Many experienced anglers are frustrated on the Delaware because they don't understand the quirks of these wild trout and the insects on which they feed. With their Advanced Guided River program, the Delaware River Club teaches how to best imitate the local insect life, making the proper approach and presentation. During this three-day comprehensive program, fishermen will fish, eat, talk and sleep trout fishing with the brain trust himself. Graduates of this school told me they have never had so much fun in the pursuit of excellence.

Guided trips are also available through the club's large guide staff. On these half- or full-day excursions, guests are floated, waded or both, depending on conditions and preferences. The river has long been renowned for its big, wild, and selective trout. Hatch-match aficionados from the world over converge here to meet the challenge of these magnificent fish.

Al and his people are all knowledgeable professionals, and pioneers in fly fishing and instruction on the upper Delaware. Their guiding techniques have been developed and perfected with thousands of individuals over every kind of fishing situation. Their understanding of fish habitats, insect life and imitation is virtually unsurpassed, and makes for a wonderful fishing experience.

the facilities

The main lodge began life as a farmhouse back in the 1830's, but now accommodates guests with four bedrooms and three bathrooms. There is a living room with a fly tying table, cable television and movies. The spacious front porch provides a beautiful view of the Home Pool with plenty of chairs to relax in and watch the fish rise. There are fourteen suites adjacent to the main lodge. These one- and two-bedroom structures feature a living room, bathroom, refrigerator, coffee maker and cable television.

A 30- by 50-foot heated swimming pool is the newest addition. A spa, sauna & exercise room, along with a tennis court are planned for the near future. These are located on a hill overlooking the resort and the river. Several hundred feet from the pool is a beautiful, spring fed trout pond with picnic benches and canoes available. These amenities are available to all guests.

Within walking distance from the Club, there are hiking and mountain bike trails. And plenty of wildlife, with sightings of eagle, black bear, deer, bobcat, wild turkey and fox a common occurrence.

The Club is part of the Delaware River Preserve (same owners), which is over 400 acres with 2 1/2 miles of private access on the West Branch. This property enjoys vistas of the southern Catskill Mountains. Limited homesites, as well as custom-built log homes, are available to the angler — all in a natural pristine environment.

the cuisine

The "private" dining room at the Delaware River Club is known for its Italian Haute cuisine. Northeastern fly fishermen and "foodies" alike list it as a favorite as do chefs, wine directors and food critics from the *New York Times* and *New York Magazine*, who come here on a regular basis.

The dining room is not open to the public. It is available only to guests of the resort and only on a limited basis. No more than thirty people per meal for breakfast, lunch and dinner, and reservations are recommended. During cocktail hour, hors d'oeuvres, Italian, Chilean and Californian wines, and a selection of beers are served.

Dinner is a six-course affair that includes appetizer, salad, main course, side dishes and dessert. Chef Fabio prepares these gourmet meals using only fresh and homemade ingredients.. The first evening I was there, we sat down to a meal fit for a king. We began with bruschetta, a Fabrizio salad, and a dish of smoked salmon with capers. Next came Risotto Milanese, made with wild mushrooms. This was followed by the main course, roasted rack of lamb with potato and asparagus. Three wines accompanied our meal, including a fantastic 1996 Vin Santo Riserva Capezzana. A selection of cheeses and fresh baked breads completed the feast.

a day in the life of…tony may and sandy bing

Tony May has been coming to the Delaware River Club for more than fifteen years now. While here, his daily ritual has evolved into a comfortable pattern. He climbs out of bed usually around 8:00 am and heads down to the restaurant for some toast and coffee.

At 9:00, he and his partner, Sandy Bing, sit down in the living room discussing the previous days events. Decisions are made as to which flies will be most effective this day. After some serious fly-tying, they suit up and head over to the Fly Shop. Here they fine tune their strategy for the day with the guides.

Then its off to reconnoiter the three river systems and decide, based on water clarity, water levels and temperature, which will be the "hot spot" for the day. Actual fishing for Tony and Sandy usually begins around 11:00 am. They will fish as long as the fish are rising, and always pack a light lunch, thus maximizing their time in the water.

They don't return to the lodge until after sunset. After taking off waders and freshening up, it's over to the dining room to enjoy Fabio's current gourmet creation. The end of the day will find Tony and Sandy enjoying a fine cigar and comparing fish stories with the other guests, while already beginning to plot the next day's moves.

guest comments

"I have traveled the world as a food journalist and an angler. The Delaware River Club, in addition to the finest trout fishing in the east, has the best cuisine of any lodge in the world. Caucci's passion for the sport and his gusto for the pleasures of the table are the order of the day at this resort."

— *Peter Kaminsky, Food Critic & Fishing Journalist for the New York Times & New York Magazine*

"Terrific fishing, great food and service, plus incredibly knowledgeable staff add up to one of the greatest fly-fishing experiences in the country."

— *Tom Valenti, Executive Chef at Ouest, New York City*

"Working in the hospitality business, I know what it means to receive outstanding service. Al Caucci and his guides are not only extremely knowledgeable and professional, they make the learning fun!"

— *Ralph Hersom, Wine Director at LeCirque, New York City*

"For the premier fishing in the northeast, head to the Delaware River. The Delaware River Club, a homey old lodge, on its most productive pools, provides excellent fly-fishing throughout the summer when other streams have warmed up. Hotelier and grand master fly rodder-in-residence is the legendary Al Caucci, who invented the elegant and dependable Comparadun."

— *New York Magazine, "Summer Fun" Issue, July 2000*

"I came expecting a basic fishing camp and found a 4-star restaurant, great rooms and a staff of some of the nicest and most knowledgeable people I have ever met."

— *Jim Perry, Vista, New York*

directions

The Delaware River Club is located in the northeastern corner of Pennsylvania, on the West Branch of the Delaware River. It took me only three hours to drive from the Philadelphia Airport, heading north on 476 through Allentown and Scranton. For detailed directions, go to their website at — www.mayfly.com.

THE FIREHOLE RANCH

the place

The rivers that tumble off the Yellowstone plateau—the Madison, Gallatin, Henry's Fork of the Snake, Gibbon and Firehole—are legendary for offering some of the best trout fishing on the continent. Located in the geographic heart of these blue ribbon trout streams, the Firehole Ranch offers an experience worthy of world-class fishing.

Nestled among towering mountains along the shores of Hebgen Lake, the Firehole Ranch defines rustic elegance. Catering to the needs of serious and novice anglers alike, the ranch has been Orvis endorsed since 1986 and was the first recipient of the coveted Orvis "Lodge of the Year Award" in 1996.

The Firehole is the kind of place that guests return to year after year. Some anglers fall into a familiar routine each year, filling their dance card with favorites like the Madison or the Henry's Fork. But for other anglers, the Firehole Ranch is the kind of place one can come for years and fish new water every day. The ranch also offers a wide variety of activities for the non-angler, including horseback riding, canoeing, mountain biking and hiking.

The first guests came to the Firehole Ranch in 1947, casting bamboo rods and filling wicker creels with the day's catch. While fishing practices have changed over the decades, the ambiance of the Firehole has endured. The log lodge still carries its original and classic lines. It is simultaneously timeless, comfortable and classy. Most of the cabins are original, and all have been updated and are well appointed.

One of the reasons that the Firehole feels intimate is that the ranch remains small, with a capacity of only twenty guests. During the peak season, they employ thirty people, which means three staff members for every couple. With this level of service, it is small wonder that a large percentage of their guests return year after year.

the people

Lynda Caine did not know that she was destined to become a guest ranch owner. Back in 1932, her grandparents built a summer place on Hebgen Lake where she spent all of her childhood summers. The family property is now in its fourth generation. In 1999, Lynda decided she wanted to raise her daughter in Montana and moved from Seattle to the cabin she helped build on her own land on Hebgen Lake.

Soon after she learned that the adjacent property, the Firehole Ranch, was up for sale. If bought by a developer this wonderful 420-acre ranch would be subdivided into twenty acre "ranchettes". She purchased the property in order to prevent the demise of this historic place and preserve the natural beauty of the land. Her goal was to keep the ranch intact and to let the small community feel remain constant in an ever-changing environment. She has succeeded.

At one time George Kimberly was an unlikely ranch manager. Once a trial lawyer in North Carolina, George and his wife decided to make a radical lifestyle change. His love of fly-fishing brought him to Montana, where he met Lynda, who quickly signed him on. George's easy way with people makes him both a great host and manager.

Jim Berkenfield, head guide, directs a professional staff of eight guides that are all expert in teaching the beginner or guiding the more experienced fishers.

the fishing

The Ranch is surrounded by world-class trout water, including the Madison, the Yellowstone, the Gallatin, Henry's Fork of the Snake River, the Gibbon and the Firehole. Hebgen Lake, a stone's throw from the lodge, provides exciting float tube fly-fishing for wild brown trout. The fish in these waters are aggressive, and can grow to between five and seven pounds. They can be fished from early June through late September.

The ranch boat ferries guests across the lake each morning, with freshly prepared lunches, to begin the day's fishing. Some of the choices include floating the Madison in a drift boat, wading the flat water of the Railroad Ranch section of the Henry's Fork, and day hikes into Yellowstone National Park (the ranch is only sixteen miles from the West entrance) to small streams teeming with cutthroat trout.

For guests who wish to fish for high mountain rainbows, nearby Coffin Lake is only a horseback ride away. An expert guide will accompany you, along with a packed picnic lunch. Tackle and flies are always available at the Orvis shop just off the main lodge.

Past Presidents and renowned fly fishermen from all over the world have flocked to these waters for nearly 100 years for the quality and quantity of fish caught on the fly. The people at Orvis agree, having stated, "You can travel around the world to fish for trout but you can't find more consistent quality trout fishing than in Firehole Ranch country."

the facilities

The Andrew Harper Collection, a highly respected authority on luxury travel, describes this resort as one of the United State's classic fishing lodges. High praise, indeed.

Continuing the tradition of style and comfort established by the great lodges of days past, the Firehole Ranch cabins are rustic, with fireplaces, carpeting, individual bathrooms and cozy sitting

areas. The cabins are located about 200 yards from the main lodge area, between the forest and meadows that reach down to the shores of Hebgen Lake. Each of these ten guest lodgings accommodates at least two people.

Meals are served in the main lodge, an original log structure highlighted by a beautiful floor-to-ceiling fireplace. The lodge is tastefully decorated with antique lamps, overstuffed couches and well-crafted wooden tables and chairs.

I actually arrived here on opening day - June 15th. After meeting some of the staff, including manager George Kimberly and his wife Karen, I decided to get settled into my cabin. I was immediately struck by the extra touches of class - from the personally addressed information folder and handwritten welcoming card to the gourmet chocolates and bottle of wine sitting on the credenza. Each cabin has a covered front porch facing Hebgen Lake and the Madison mountain range, and a rear porch looking into the wooded areas that surround the ranch. Both porches were adorned with beautifully kept flowers and plants. The view from the cabin was full of Montana sky, snow-capped mountains, and white pelicans skimming the waters of Hebgen Lake.

For those who feel like pursuing other leisure activities, the ranch maintains a small herd of saddle-ready horses. The ranch also has canoes for exploring the nearby coves of Hebgen Lake, and mountain bikes for exploring the trails on the ranch and in adjacent Gallatin National Forest. Hiking the trails is also a popular option to view the wildlife and the numerous species of wildflowers and plants.

the cuisine

Fine dining is one of the hallmarks of this resort. Chefs Bruno and Kris Georgeton, employed by the Ranch for fourteen years, provide a world-class culinary experience for the guests. Bruno began his career as a teenager in France. He later worked in Washington, D.C., and eventually moved west where he met his wife Kris, who was an Executive Chef in Jackson, Wyoming.

Breakfast includes eggs, bacon, pancakes, omelets, and waffles. Evenings begin with cocktails and hors d'oeuvres at the elegant mahogany bar. Dinners are served in a glass-walled verandah overlooking the lake.

When sitting down to dinner on my first evening, I saw a menu specially printed for that day's fare. It read like a five-star restaurant. We began with Organic Baby Greens with toasted almonds, duck confit and fresh raspberries. The main course demanded a decision. Either Fresh Alaskan Halibut sautéed and served on a bed of beluga lentils with a lemon beurre blanc; or Rocky Mountain Elk Chop pan seared, with rosemary and dried cherry demi-glace. Thoughtfully chosen wines selected to accompany the entrées are offered each evening. Dessert featured a Coffee Cheesecake with white chocolate sauce.

One night each week an outdoor barbeque is held on the patio and lawn overlooking Hebgen Lake. Features include grilled salmon and steaks, homemade salads and deserts, and western folk music performed by a live band.

a day in the life of...the brooks family

John and Carol Brooks, with their son Bob and daughter Margi live in Indiana. They first came here on vacation back in 1990. They haven't missed a year since! You realize how keen they are about this place when told the details of their journey door to door. Up at 5:00 am, they leave their home at 6:00 am, then take three flights and a rental car ride — arriving at the resort just after 6:00 pm.

Each day, they meet for breakfast around 7:30 am. Then it's back to their cabins to gather up the necessary gear for the day. The boat then takes them across the water to rendezvous with the fishing guides. Choices are many, including floating, wading or fishing the lake. Sometime after noon, they will stop for lunch as a group, relax a while and trade fishing stories — first fish, biggest fish, and most fish. Always entertaining.

The last shuttle back to the lodge leaves at 5:30 pm. The family will usually fish right up to this point, sometimes scrambling to get back in time.

Then it's back to the cabins, clean up a little, and head over to the main lodge for drinks and dinner. The end of the day will find them along with the other guests trading tall tales — who caught what, where and when. Finally it is time to sit and seriously plan the next day's fishing activities.

guest comments

"We had a glorious time. The care and feeding of your customers is absolutely first rate, with every member of your staff deserving a medal of excellence for their service and friendly attitude. In business, I have traveled to a lot of places and can say without reservation that Firehole Ranch is a ten-star place on a five-star system. The rooms were wonderful, our guide excellent, and the food beyond expectations. Everything is so well organized to make guests feel like royalty. Thanks so much for a truly memorable time."

— *Bob & Liz H., Massachusetts*

"As of this date, we have made twenty-seven trips to the Firehole Ranch since 1988. That in itself says a great deal about how pleased we are with our experience here. The accommodations, food, fishing, service, and all the people who make it run so smoothly are "five star."

— *Richard & Phyllis N., Sioux Falls, South Dakota*

"Firehole Ranch has my vote for the best operation I have seen in thirty years of fishing all over."

— *Gordon R., Gig Harbor, Washington*

"I will leave this place in absolute awe. I can honestly say this was a full package experience. It was the best fishing expedition that I have ever had in my life. It is hard to believe that a place like this really exists. Thank you all for my incredible experience."

— *Michael F., Dover, New Hampshire*

directions

Most travelers to the Firehole fly to Salt Lake City, then take a Delta Connection to West Yellowstone. The ranch has a free shuttle service from the airport. If you are driving, I would suggest leaving your car at the Kirkwood Marina on Hwy 287. You will be picked up by boat and ferried to the doorstep of the Ranch. If you choose to drive to the lodge as I did, do so slowly. The last fifteen miles are gravel road. Ten miles into my journey I came around a bend and barely missed two deer bounding across it. For more information, go to their website at — www.fireholeranch.com.

ALASKA'S
FISHING UNLIMITED LODGE

the place

Fishing in the Iliamna region of Alaska is diverse — rainbows topping the scales in double digits, all five species of Pacific Salmon, Arctic Char, Grayling, plus the opportunity to fish innumerable lakes, rivers and mountain streams.

This is Alaska's Bristol Bay watershed, a 30,000-square-mile-expanse that is known the world over for its fishing. It includes the Iliamna/Kvichak drainage, Katmai and Lake Clark National Parks and Kodiak Island.

Located in a protected cove in the Lake Clark National Park is Alaska's Fishing Unlimited Lodge. They have two modern wood and glass lodges, which offer great views of the 4000-foot Tanalian Peak and the surrounding wilderness.

The resort sits on five acres of forested lakeside land. Dining is in one lodge while the other is used as a recreational facility, with a pool table, a fly-tying room, various games, a television and plenty of room to stretch out and relax.

Your journey begins as mine did, with a lodge representative meeting you at Lake Clark Air, located on Merrill Field in downtown Anchorage. The weather on the morning of my flight was perfect. The trip through Lake Clark Pass is simply unforgettable. You weave your way through monstrous mountains and glacial fields until you descend over Lake Clark and land on the airstrip located adjacent to the lodge.

the people

The lodge is owned and operated by Merrill "Woody" Wood. Growing up in northern Maine gave him his first taste of the great outdoors. His love of the wilderness and the sport of fishing had brought Woody to the state of Alaska several times over the preceding decades. Combine that with his background in aviation and it is no wonder that, in January of 2001, he seized on an opportunity to purchase a premiere fishing lodge, complete with four airplanes — the Fishing Unlimited Lodge.

This place gives new meaning to "family run" business. During my visit in July, I met two of his sons, Bob and Pat, his daughter-in-law Nancy and several of his grandchildren. All were helping maintain the smooth operation of the lodge.

Their chief pilot and guide is Dave Tyson. He has been here since shortly after it opened in 1976. The other pilot guides have all been here five years or more. Dave's wife, Debbie, keeps all the guests well fed by running the entire food operation for the lodge.

the fishing

The fishing at this resort is simply amazing. You can catch a forty-five pound King Salmon one day, and fly fish for trophy Rainbow trout the next. Kings, the largest of the Pacific Salmon, start their run in mid-June and go through mid-July. The Sockeye and Chum salmon runs also start about the second week of June. The Coho salmon arrive in early August and remain through September. Trophy rainbow fishing opens the first of June and continues on through the entire season.

Trophy Rainbow trout fishing generally is the best in early June and again in late August through early October. These late season rainbows are especially fat, having feasted on salmon smolt and eggs during the summer.

Fishing Unlimited believes that the best way for their guests to experience all aspects of the Bristol Bay region is to fly you out to a host of different locales every day. To accomplish this, they employ a small fleet of airplanes. Two DeHavilland Beaver and two Cessna 206s give you access to any area at any time you want. The pilots are also highly qualified fishing guides, and stay with you to offer the ultimate in freedom and flexibility.

The Lodge also has sixteen strategically placed boats, which allow their fishers to cover a large expanse of water in search of the best possible fishing experience. They also offer a variety of float trips that take you to seldom fished rivers and streams.

Many lodges manage guests by scheduling them to certain rivers on specific days. Not so here. Numbers are kept small, so pilot, guide and guest are together for the duration of the stay. Each evening, you and the

staff have a sit-down, and discuss the areas you'd like to fish, and what fish you would like to catch. Since opening, the lodge's pilots and guides have kept detailed ongoing journals. These are invaluable reference sources for you when deciding where to go.

Because they do their best to minimize their impact on this pristine landscape, a strict catch-and-release policy is enforced on all freshwater fish. With salmon however, it is a different story. You keep all your daily limits if you wish, and the lodge will vacuum pack, freeze and box it up for you to take home.

the facilities

Spacious cedar cabins are the anglers' home while here. Each cabin features a private bath and is fully equipped to provide a comfortable home away from home. Wooden boardwalks connect the cabins to both lodges, the wood-fired saunas and the hot tubs.

After a hard day's fishing, it was fun to return to my cabin and find some really nice added touches, such as ice for cocktails and a fresh appetizer. Everything here is geared toward giving you two things — unlimited fishing opportunities and unparalleled hospitality.

Although great fishing is the primary goal of most people, the trip is about far more than just fishing. Since you fly out every day, you are able to explore and experience the sheer beauty and vastness of Alaska. Its scenery and diversity of landscape is without equal.

Wildlife not seen in most parts of the planet abound here. Most common are brown and black bear, caribou, moose, Dall sheep, Bald eagles, wolf and tundra swans. When you are flying along the coast, chances of spotting sea lions, sea otters or whales are better than even.

leisure pursuits

Although fishing is the main focus at this place, they also feature non-fishing excursions. More than a few of the guests are thrilled with the opportunity of observing the beauty that is Alaska. Some of the activities include getting up-close and personal with the caribou herds, digging clams on the beach, bear watching, and exploring the sea coast. You can also land on a lake in the crater of a volcano. That experience will probably be a first. They also offer an exploration of the Land of 10,000 Smokes.

For those guests who choose to really see Alaska, the resort offers programs that range from float trips to hiking and photography sessions.

the cuisine

As great chefs everywhere know, presentation is one key to fine dining. At Fishing Unlimited, the menu is hearty, the food delicious and the presentation as nice as that found in any four-star gourmet restaurant. A typical weekly menu might include King crab, grilled New York Strip steak, freshly-caught salmon, halibut, barbecued baby back ribs and a selection of Italian, Mexican and Chinese dishes. The breads, rolls and desserts are all homemade and always fresh.

A full breakfast is served at 6:00 am. It will usually include blueberry sourdough pancakes, omelets made to order, bacon and freshly baked applesauce muffins. Because you are out for most of the day, lunch is either packed into coolers or served up fresh as a shore lunch.

On the evening of my visit, the appetizer was a plate of large shrimp cooked in minced garlic butter and Southwest spices. The main course featured grilled New York steak that had been marinated in oil, soy sauce, garlic and vinegar. This was served with baked potato, sauteed mushrooms and steamed asparagus rolled in egg and garlic butter. For dessert, appropriately enough, they offered Baked Alaska.

After years of being asked for their "secret" recipes, the chefs here relented and published a cookbook called, "Fishing Unlimited Lodge Alaskan Appetites." After all, you will need to know how to cook all that salmon you'll be taking home.

a day in the life of…dr. hugh sheffield

Hugh and his wife, Peggy traveled here from their home in Houston, Texas. Their day starts early, usually around 5:30 am. They go over to the lodge for breakfast at 6:00 am, then back to the cabin to suit up for the day. Fly out is shortly thereafter, where they will fish several hot spots selected by their pilot guide.

Come five o'clock in the afternoon, it's back to the lodge, then up to their cabin to shower and change. After joining the other guests for cocktails and appetizers at 6:30 pm, dinner is served. They usually call it a day a little after 9:00 pm, and are asleep within the hour.

guest comments

"Fifth and best trip yet. I caught more fish than I could ever want, was pampered by the warmest staff and shared it with my son and nephew. Doesn't get any better."

— *Kim Junbe, Celebration, Florida*

"Fabulous – extraordinary – outstanding – first class. It was a pleasure to join the Fishing Unlimited family."

—*Manfred Neuss, Calabasas, California*

"Formidable et magnifique et excellent."

— *Pierre and Yvette Bonelle, Boulogne, France*

"Once again, too good to be true. See you all next year."

— *Bob Mead, Cumbria, England*

directions

Fishing Unlimited is in the heart of Lake Clark National Park and Preserve near Port Alsworth. The lodge is approximately 160 miles southwest of Anchorage. Their chartered flights will bring you directly from Anchorage to the lodge in a scenic one-hour flight. For more information visit their website at — www.alaskalodge.com.

FLATHEAD LAKE LODGE

the place

Flathead Lake is located adjacent to the Bob Marshall Wilderness Area and the Jewel Basin Primitive Area. It is named after the Flathead Indians who still live on the reservation on the south end of the lake. The lake measures thirty miles long and fifteen miles wide. The water is comfortable for swimming, yet pure enough to drink. Flathead Lake is so vast, the horizon blends from water into mountain in one smooth stroke. The mountain ranges and unspoiled forests make for a stunning backdrop.

On 2,000 acres of timbered ranch country in northern Montana, just south of Glacier National Park and the Canadian border, you will find the famous Averill's Flathead Lake Lodge. It is nestled in a secluded bay that sits at an elevation of 3,000 feet above sea level.

A working dude ranch since 1945, Flathead Lake Lodge is unique in its location, perched directly on the shores of the largest natural lake west of the Great Lakes. Western atmosphere abounds, from the cowboys who work on the ranch every day of the year to the log-cabin style accommodations and ample outdoor activities.

This place brings to life the cowboys, horses, cattle, dudes and rodeos from the books and movies about the old west. It is truly a look back at history. The surrounding countryside offers exceptionally scenic rides down century-old trails.

Flathead Lake Lodge has been featured in over eighty national publications, including *Better Homes & Gardens, Sunset, Travel, Travel & Leisure* and *Bon Appetit*. The lodge is consistently rated in the "top ten" family vacations in America. *Elite Magazine* selected Averill's as one of the country's top three dude ranches. And recently, *Diversions Magazine* chose this place as "One of the five most unique family vacations anywhere."

the people

This ranch began life in 1932 as a boy's camp. Les Averill, who grew up on the lake, found the property vacant after returning home from the war. His boyhood dream was to build and operate a ranch. Les and his wife, Dolores, worked hard to build this place into a remote family vacation destination. Their efforts spanned a quarter of a century, from 1945 to 1970. The ranch slowly began attracting people from around the world. Dignitaries, celebrities and families discovered the Montana hideaway and word rapidly spread. After thirty years of success, Les retired and passed on the operation to four of his sons. Doug Averill has operated the ranch since 1971.

In the beginning, it operated as a Western retreat for vacationers travelling from the East via railroad who were looking to return to a simpler time. Doug and his team have been successful in keeping it that way. The ranch offers guests what it always has — the opportunity to enjoy a real western vacation and hospitality in an unparalleled setting.

Their friendly and proficient staff is made up of college students from all across the country. I found their youthful enthusiasm and exuberance to be instantly contagious.

the fishing

Well more than half the visitors to Flathead Lake Lodge have been here before. This ranch has, over the years, become so popular that they now boast a return rate topping seventy percent. That is a significant figure in this industry.

A key ingredient to this success is the tremendous fishing to be found. Species of fish in the area include rainbow and brook trout, silver salmon, cutthroat trout, Dolly Varden and Mackinaw. The latter two have been known to reach a staggering forty-five pounds. Most fisherman enjoy spending their time on this mammoth lake. The more adventuresome fish the countless rivers and streams nearby.

Montana enjoys a well-deserved reputation for being a fly fisherman's nirvana. And the lodge can accommodate anglers of all skill levels, from beginner to world class. You can go it alone, or the folks here will be happy to provide you with a guide knowledgeable in the local tried-and-true techniques.

Marv Bielski has been guiding guests here for more than two decades. Growing up in Grayling, Michigan, his dad taught him to fly fish when he was only seven. His love of the sport has stayed with him ever since. He, and his expertise are available all season, save for a ten-day guide trip he takes to Alaska each year with ranch guests who want an Alaskan experience.

the facilities

Flathead Lake Lodge is large enough to accommodate a variety of groups. They feature large log lodges and individual family cottages. Their total capacity at any given time is 120 guests. Meals are served in the historic main lodge or on the patio overlooking the lake, weather permitting.

They have one of the most magnificent lodges I've seen in my travels throughout North America. Built using whole logs of tamarack, it features thirty-five-foot vaulted ceilings, skylights and classic pane windows everywhere. The massive stone fireplace soars floor to ceiling. It is so large, the mantel is a full eight feet above the floor. Hardwood floors and hand-hewn timber furniture complete the elegantly rustic effect.

The lodge has four meeting rooms that are popular as a corporate getaway or conference. These rooms can house over a hundred people comfortably, and on occasion one group will completely take over the ranch. All meeting rooms come with soft seating, complete amenities and views of the lake. There are also some suites and break-away rooms available.

I was booked into a room in the main lodge. Expecting something fairly small, relative to the family cottages, I was amazed to enter my room and find a tastefully appointed loft suite, complete with log beam ceiling and sliding glass doors onto a deck overlooking the lake. As with the rest of the lodge, wood is everywhere, down to the four-poster queen bed.

The Averill family has developed the property into a complete destination resort. There is a beach, complete with canoes, kayaks and a fleet of boats. You'll also find a rodeo arena, horses, tennis courts, nearby golf courses, and enough planned activities to guarantee boredom is not an option.

leisure pursuits

In addition to the fishing, the incredible collection of outdoor activities is where the Flathead Lake Lodge separates itself from the crowd.

White water raft trips leave every morning for excursions down the Flathead River. Sailboats are available for gliding across the Flathead Lake. The lake is also the perfect place for those who want to water ski. At the day's end, there is an evening cruise that winds up the river to the water fowl preserve, where you will see the majestic Bald eagle and osprey.

There are four hard-surfaced tennis courts, and with no resident professional, games are always leisurely. Every week, those keen on the sport can participate in the Cowboy Classic Tennis Tournament. Other special events include a cocktail cruise, a cookout in the mountains, or a sailboat race between the two historic fifty-foot Q-class sloops, Questa and Nor'Easter, moored at the docks.

The surrounding mountain country provides hours of trail riding time for guests all the way down to six years of age. The choice of horseback rides includes a morning breakfast ride, a steak fry ride, a day-long ride and an evening ride. Wranglers who have a way with both horses and children are always available for supervision. A children's rodeo and cowboy steer roping takes place each week.

And, in the tradition of days past, guests can lend a hand in the daily ranch chores, from the training of colts to feeding and watering the livestock. The ranch offers a private game preserve complete with with trophy elk and buffalo.

the cuisine

Early morning breakfast rides are very popular. There is something about preparing and eating breakfast out in the forest sitting by an open fire.

Barbecue is what they do best here. Prime meats cooked slowly over an open flame, and served family style in the huge main dining room. Homemade breads, pies and preserves made from Montana berries accent the authentic Western cooking. Often, the preserves are actually made from berries hand-picked by guests of the ranch.

The evening of my arrival they served up a sumptuous supper. We started with a spinach salad, with grapes, blue cheese and a champagne vinaigrette dressing. The main course was roasted duck, with a delicious orange sesame glaze. Wild rice and baked acorn squash accompanied. Dessert featured homemade cheesecake with a fresh peach sauce. The atmosphere is informal and casual.

guest comments

"I would like to express the sincere appreciation of the Committee members, spouses and staff for the wonderful experience we recently had at the lodge. The meals, rides, the meeting room, the cruise — everything was just superb. Of course, apart from the beautiful site and facility, the most important element was the friendly and helpful staff. Thank you so much for all your help in planning the events and for all the assistance we received while we were there. I hope that we can come back again in the near future.

— *Abel J. Mattos, Administrative Office of the United States Courts, June 2002*

"How and where does one begin to thank you for your extreme generosity and hospitality? I can't tell you how much we enjoyed a relaxing week here in this most gorgeous natural setting! Our accommodations were more than twice the space needed. The very nicely decorated rooms were full of great amenities. As for the food, it was just this side of heaven."

— *Pat & Woody (Ken) Woodhouse, 2002*

directions

As remote as it sounds, this ranch is very easy to get to. It is accessible by road, located just off Montana Highway 35, a mere fifteen minutes south of Kalispell. If you are flying in, land at the Glacier Park International Airport, located only thirty minutes away. Shuttle service is always available. For more detailed information visit their website at — www.averills.com.

HAWK LAKE LODGE

the place

Ontario's most beautiful and rugged wilderness is found in the Canadian Shield. The land is legendary for its clear waters, amazing rock formations and variety of high quality fishing experiences.

Part of this legend is the Hawk Lake Lodge. When this premier wilderness facility first opened its doors back in 1986, it was immediately heralded as one of Ontario's highest rated fishing lodges. Carefully designed as a private retreat for only twenty-four guests at a time, this resort offers not only the wilderness and solitude sought after by so many, but a great angling adventure. This includes access to some of the best, unspoiled, light tackle sportfishing lakes in Canada.

Sitting on a peninsula at the north end of Hawk Lake, the lodge is surrounded by heavily wooded grounds. The main lodge is a wonderfully crafted log building featuring a reception area, tackle and fly shop, guest dining room with polished maple floors, floor-to-ceiling granite fireplace, a lounge and library area with a wall of windows overlooking Hawk Lake.

the people

There is an old adage — life begins at forty. In the case of Garry and Sandy Delton it is fact. As a young couple they followed in the path of millions before them. They got educated, got married, started a family and began to acquire the standard material possessions. But something was missing.

After many serious discussions, it was discovered that they both wanted one thing — to live and work in the wilderness. With that in mind, they began to head north, looking for that perfect spot. They found it when they reached the edge of the Canadian Shield, in western Ontario.

Here, in 1985, Garry and Sandy carved out a new life for themselves when they built the Hawk Lake Lodge. They spend their days working with the call of the loon, not the honk of the horn; enjoying the clean fresh air with no distractions like telephones or televisions; meeting people they never would have met if they hadn't taken the road less traveled. All this is living proof that their vision is now reality.

the fishing

Hawk Lake Lodge is open from mid-May through early September. It is the only lodge on this system of twenty pristine lakes. Whether you want to spin cast, bait cast or fly fish, they offer some of the finest fast-action smallmouth bass, Northern pike, lake trout and trophy walleye fishing available anywhere in Canada. The diversity of lakes here virtually guarantees a quality angling experience in any season.

You are encouraged to fish the many portage lakes. Clean portage trails range from 150 feet to 3800 feet. Boats and motors are waiting at every lake — all you need to take is your fishing gear and lunch.

In an effort to share the wealth of knowledge that they have acquired about the lake system, the staff provided us an "on-the-water" orientation tour of Hawk Lake shortly after we arrived. During the tour, they discussed with us what the different lakes had to offer and where the fishing was currently "hot." Also covered was what baits to use and the presentations that have been most productive. They have even mapped and depth charted all the lakes.

Of the fish species abundant here, the one I had never fished for was the Smallmouth bass. At a small, wind-protected lake adjacent to Hawk Lake, I put my line in the water. Discussions with my guide had revealed that these fast-action acrobats are best caught with light tackle, like a 5-weight fly fishing rod. It was good advice. In one session spanning four hours, I caught no less than fifteen Smallmouth bass. And although there were no trophy fish that day, they ranged in size from sixteen to nineteen inches. Large enough to set the hook into my fishing future.

the facilities

Placed strategically throughout the property are ten private guest cabins. They are all comfortable, spacious and tastefully furnished. Each cabin has at least one full private bath and is carpeted and heated. Some of the amenities include windows looking out to the lake, large well-furnished living rooms, ceiling fans, refrigerators and lakeside decks. The cabins range from one- to four-bedroom design.

My cabin was right at the water's edge. I could, if so inclined, cast out to rising fish right from my porch. When I first arrived, it was a real treat to find a welcome basket of fresh fruit and snacks sitting on the coffee table. There was even a supply of soft drinks in the fridge.

The main lodge is open from 7:00 am to 10:00 pm. They have a large library of books, games, puzzles and video cassettes there for the asking. And coffee and snacks are always "on" here.

At least half the guests took advantage of the outdoor hot tub and sauna after a long hard day fighting fish. For those health-conscious people, the lodge has provided a complete fitness center, including Cybex and Lifestyler bikes, Precor treadmill and Pulse Fitness weight equipment. I chose a more leisurely pace, and played eight-ball on their regulation pool table.

leisure pursuits

While the primary reason most folks come here is the fishing, the place has a great selection of other leisure activities. There are walking trails and old logging roads for those who like to hike through remote wilderness. They also have all the latest sports equipment for those guests who enjoy biking or canoeing.

Within a thirty mile radius, you will find native art on sale, a sheep farm where you can watch them shearing before checking out their wonderful woolen products. There is even a mid-day and evening tour boat cruise of Lake of the Woods, along with a local casino and a golf course.

the cuisine

Breakfast is served here between 7:30 am and 8:30 am. There is a "breakfast bar", with everything from fresh fruit and cereals to biscuits with sausage gravy. After beginning your repast here, you order the main event. Choices are many, and include the daily chef's special, eggs, pancakes, french toast, bacon, sausage and potatoes. For the truly avid angler, they offer a "take with" breakfast. This is delivered to your cabin the night before, allowing you an early start on the water.

There are three options for lunch. The traditional Canadian shore lunch - fresh caught fish with onions, potatoes, beans and corn. Fruits and cookies are dessert. They also offer a specially prepared picnic lunch, or a return to the lodge for salad, soup and sandwich.

Around 5:00 pm, the bar is open and everyone meets for cocktails, hors d'oeuvres and "fish stories."

Dinner is served anytime between 6:00 pm and 7:00 pm. I sat down just before seven, after a long day on the water. We began with homemade soup and fresh-baked bread, along with a trip to the salad table. The main entree was crispy-skinned Roast Duck, served with a delicious black cherry puree sauce, wild rice pilaf and sliced carrots al dente. I had to pass on dessert, which featured a selection of sinful treats, including a double chocolate cake and multi-colored fruit flan.

guest comments

"You never fail us! Disneyland of the North woods! Really great."

— Kay & Glynn Morris, Playa del Rey, California

"I now know what lies at the end of a fisherman's rainbow — that little glimpse of heaven known as Hawk Lake Lodge."

— Jay Sidmore, Aurora, Illinois

"I didn't think it was possible…every year something new…every year a little bit better…its been a great eleven years! I am looking forward to many more!"

— Mike Kukla, Schaumburg, Illinois

"I did not think that it could be better than I could imagine. It was!"

— Mike Crosett, Tallahassee, Florida

directions

The lodge is located twenty-eight miles east of Kenora, Ontario in Canada. It is 150 miles east of Winnipeg, Manitoba and 125 miles north of International Falls, Minnesota. From the major U.S. airports, commercial flight connections can be made into Kenora or Winnipeg. Currently Northwest services both Canadian cities and International Falls. For more detailed information visit their website at — www.hawk-lake.com.

KROGS KAMP ON THE KENAI

the place

Krog's Kamp is located on the banks of the beautiful Kenai River near Soldotna and offers first class fishing on Alaska's Kenai Peninsula. Along with great fishing and deluxe accommodations you will find genuine old-time Alaskan hospitality.

Accommodations run the gamut from rustic to deluxe. There are large chalets overlooking the river and quaint cabins nestled in the woods. There is a gazebo out near the river's edge where guests can just kick back and relax and watch the river flow by, join a group around the nearby campfire, or really mellow out in the sauna or hot tub. There is also a new fitness cabin offering an exercise regime that will keep you on track.

Krog's Kamp on The Kenai River is one of the few resorts in this corner of the world that is open year round. Summer activities include, of course, fishing for king salmon, red and silver salmon, dolly varden, trophy rainbow trout and barn door-sized halibut. During the winter months, you will find residents and guests snow machining, glacier skiing, cross country skiing, dog sledding and ice fishing in nearby lakes.

My drive from Anchorage took just over two-and-a-half hours. It will probably take three hours for the vacationer traveling here as there is so much spectacular scenery and wildlife to see on the way that photographs are not an option, they are mandatory.

the people

Long time Alaskans, Mel and Bob Krogseng, built this resort with the idea of sharing a wonderful part of Alaska with their guests from around the world. They met and married in Michigan in 1965 while they were both in the Air Force. Mel was a flight nurse and Bob was a radar intercept officer in the F101 Voodoo Fighter jet.

In 1970, a new fighter squadron was to be based in Alaska. Bob and Mel were offered and accepted a transfer here. Two years later, after creating an organization to help the MIAs and POWs of the Vietnam war, they decided to invite some of the children of these servicemen to Alaska to enjoy a two-week graduation trip that

dad couldn't give but Alaskans could. This trip included a two-day float trip on the Kenai River. One taste of this wild and beautiful area, with the clear turquoise waters against a backdrop of forests and snow-capped mountains was enough to change the course of their life.

Within a few months of Bob's retirement from the service, they purchased a four-acre piece of riverfront property. It has evolved over the last two decades into what it is today — a first-class fishing destination resort.

the fishing

The most popular activity during the summer is King salmon fishing which begins in May and concludes the end of July. Elusive as they are, these trophy fish are more of a challenge than any other species of Pacific salmon. Sockeye salmon start in mid-June and continue through the end of July and silvers begin in late July and continue through September.

As is often the case, rainbow trout are hot on the trail of spawning salmon. A float fishing trip on the upper Kenai River for trophy rainbows is a popular choice among the avid fishermen who visit this place, especially fly fishermen.

A few short miles away in Cook Inlet, you can fish for massive halibut. These ocean giants are some of the finest fish for the dinner table you will find anywhere. Every year, halibut are hauled aboard from these waters that weigh over 200 pounds; and, it's not uncommon to limit out early. Hooking a 200-plus pound, man-sized fish, is a thrill. One that gets better each time the story is told.

Fourteen miles to the south, a glacial-fed river, the Kasilof, is also known for its excellent fishing opportunities. A drift fishing trip for King salmon on the Kasilof provides another unique opportunity at harvesting Alaska's wild salmon stock. This river also offers some of the best bank fishing in the area for king, red and silver salmon.

In May of 1985, Soldotna resident Les Andersen won powerful bragging rights when he caught the world-record king salmon while fishing the Kenai River. It weighed in at a staggering ninety-seven pounds, four ounces.

Within five minutes of my arrival, as a group of us were standing on the banks of the river, one of the kamp boats pulled up with a guest standing in it gamely holding aloft a sixty-five pound king salmon. As I was looking in awe at this spectacle, another guest looked over and told me about the fish he caught the day before — a halibut topping the scales at 245 pounds.

the facilities

The Main House is open to all guests during their stay, and comes complete with kitchen and dining facilities, a game and reading area, computer station for guests, fax, television, video tapes, and VCR.

Three attached townhouse-style chalets sit near the river's edge. Each stands two stories, and has two full baths, complete kitchen, large living room, dining room, covered deck and gas barbecue grill. One even has a wood stove and sauna offering the ultimate in comfort.

Deluxe chalets are spread out among the trees. These two-bedroom beauties are also fully equipped, including gas log fireplaces, decks and gas barbecues. They are nicely appointed, wonderfully comfortable and designed to accommodate up to four people. The rustic cabins and bungalows, while smaller, also boast top quality amenities. In this area you will find picnic tables, a firepit, and the spa area.

During my stay, while talking with the twenty-seven guests that Mel and Bob were hosting, I discovered that nearly all of them were repeat visitors. Some of them have been coming here for five, six and seven years.

leisure pursuits

Outdoor pursuits are a natural choice for people who visit this area. In summer, camping, hiking, canoeing, wildlife viewing, birding and horseback riding are a few of the activities enjoyed. Another popular activity is sea kayaking. At Seward, you can kayak around the many fjords in Resurrection Bay. This fantastic excursion will provide many wonderful photo opportunities.

During winter months, cross-country skiing and snow-machining on groomed trails are very popular. You can also take a flight-seeing trip in a small aircraft over the amazing Harding Icefield or a float plane trip to a secluded wilderness area. If you happen to be here in April, you can drive a few miles to Cook Inlet and witness the brief stopover of thousands of snow geese on their northern migration. In early May, there are thousands of shore birds transiting the area. There is even a "Shore Bird Festival" down the road a ways in Homer.

the cuisine

The food fare at Krog's is always hearty, wholesome and delicious. Breakfast often features wild lingonberry pancakes or waffles, eggs, reindeer sausage and a variety of fresh fruits and juices. Lunch is usually packed into coolers for the fisherman to eat when they're on the water; or if eating in Kamp, will include a tasty homemade soup and sandwiches.

In the evening, drinks and hors d'oeuvres begin around 6:30 pm (fishing trips usually conclude around six o'clock). The appetizers are popular and include morsels like "teriyaki salmon backs" — tender meat next to the backbone; and "salmon balls", a whipped combination of smoked salmon, pecans and cream cheese.

We sat down to dine at 7:00 o'clock. Dinner began with a Kenai Caesar Salad followed with Mel's Halibut Olympia — filets are buttered in mayonnaise, coated with Japanese bread crumbs and put on a bed of sauteed onions, then into a super-hot oven for twelve minutes. This was served with buttered parsley egg noodles and broccoli with hollandaise sauce. Dessert featured a New York-style cheesecake topped with a raspberry sauce that was made from the local harvest of wild raspberries.

a day in the life of…glenn kriske

When I met with Glenn, the first thing he told me was that this is his seventh consecutive year coming here. This year, as usual, he brought his two sons, Jeremy and Brandon, and a dozen customers of his firm. He gets up around 5:00 am and immediately heads over to breakfast. Fishing hours are from six to six. At the end of the day, he comes back to the lodge and joins in the festivities.

After dinner, everyone sits around the fire and enjoys a glass or two of fabulous Merlot. This group has an affinity for specific vintages that Glenn brings with him. He will usually call it a day by 10:00 pm. Tomorrow and its new adventures, after all, come early.

guest comments

"Mel, simply put, you, your staff and Krogs Kamp are "King of the Kenai." No better place to be.

— *Dean Tellinghuisen, Anaheim Hills, California, July, 2002*

"In life experiences, my fishing vacation at Krogs on the Kenai ranks second only to the birth of my son."

— *Rob Simonelli, Long Beach, California, June, 2002*

directions

Fly to Anchorage, Alaska. From there, drive south on the Seward Highway. Once you reach the turnoff for Soldotna, you are about an hour away from the resort. You will pass through Cooper Landing and then Sterling. At this point, you are about seventeen miles from Soldotna. When you reach Soldotna, take a right onto the Kenai Spur Highway. Approximately $1^3/_4$ miles from the light, Big Eddy Road cuts off to the left. Once on Big Eddy, go exactly one mile down and look to your left for the Krog's Kamp sign. For more information, visit their website at — www.krogskamp.com.

MINOR BAY LODGE

the place

Anglers have flocked to the Canadian Province of Saskatchewan for decades. Close proximity to the United States, favorable exchange rates and massive fish in the innumerable lakes all combine to create fishing safaris par excellence.

In the midst of this pristine wilderness region is Wollaston Lake, Canada's thirteenth largest fresh water lake covering 1,305 square miles of area. Its crystal clear cobalt waters are an 800-square-mile fish factory, especially for monster pike. Trophy Northern pike exceeding fifty inches are the main draw; lake trout weighing more than forty pounds; walleye that have been known to grow to thirty inches and feisty Arctic grayling all abound in this huge, sparsely populated province.

Minor Bay Lodge and Outposts sits on the shores of Wollaston Lake. For the true adventurer, the outposts are located on smaller lakes around Wollaston, lakes that are reserved for exclusive use of the lodge and its guests. Among the waters available are Simpson Lake, Spence Lake and McDonald River. For the diehard fisherman, the outposts could be the calling. Fishing programs are unstructured, and anglers can fish as much or as little as they want.

the people

The managing partner that oversees Minor Bay and their other three resorts is Randy Duvell. Born and raised in Winnipeg, Manitoba, he spent many years in the commodities brokerage business. In 1986, looking to change gears and lifestyles, he left that industry to become the on-site operations manager of a fishing resort situated on God's Lake. A couple of years later he moved to a new resort that the company he was employed by was developing in Northern Manitoba. There he met and developed a friendship with Tom Smith, one of the resort's guests. Tom was interested in snow goose hunting - specifically on the coast of the Hudson Bay. As chance would have it, Kaska Goose Lodge came on the market in 1994. Tom and Randy joined forces to purchase Kaska. And thus the seeds were planted in what would grow to become Great White North Wilderness Resorts.

Minor Bay is managed by Fred Tully. After spending fifteen years in sales management, Fred decided to act on his lifelong dream and, in 1994 became the manager of a fishing and hunting lodge in Manitoba. Three years later, through contacts made at that job, he had an opportunity to become a partner with this new and growing company. He took it.

The people here are all professionals, and take pride in making sure that you have the ultimate fishing adventure. From the shore staff that keeps your cabin spotless; the chef, Loretta, who continuously treats you to new gourmet delights; servers who learn and remember individual preferences; to the bartender who remembers that you like two olives in your dry martini.

the fishing

During the summer, when I visited Minor Bay the northern pike — of the three to four foot-plus variety — were most often found in "cabbage beds," patches of pond weed that are excellent hunting grounds for these game fish. The beds are not small, often more than 100 feet long and wide, and can get extremely thick, making working flies and lures quite a challenge. The good news is that often there are so many pike in a single bed that the fly or lure is attacked within seconds of landing, making long retrieves unnecessary or even impossible, because the fly is taken before it has a chance to get too far. One such tale of cabbage bed fishing involves a three-hour battle with more than fifty Northerns, more than a dozen of which ran from forty-one to forty-seven inches.

The fantastic fishing at Minor Bay Lodge is a testament to the success of the catch and release program. In 2001, guests caught and then released more than twice the trophy pike than were caught just two years previously. And the numbers of large pike both seen and caught has increased every year since 1996, when they bought the lodge. Each and every year since then, at least two pike over fifty inches have been caught and released by Minor Bay's guests. A fifty-three inch monster — a Saskatchewan record — was caught and released in July of 2000.

Another reason for the continuing improvement in the fishing is the guides. They work hard for every angler to ensure the finest fishing experience possible. Whether you are a spin fisherman, a fly fisherman or prefer trolling the depths for those fat lakers, you'll find it here. If you come here as a fly fisherman, you are in luck. This is an Orvis-endorsed lodge, and all their guides have been fully trained in the art of fly fishing.

For those wishing to experience the adventure and variety of flying out to a remote lake, the lodge offers daily fly-outs. Their Beaver floatplane sits at the dock alongside the fourteen boats, available to those who choose to explore other lakes in the region. I was content to go out fishing on Wollaston Lake with my guide, Kerry. On our first day out, in the first hour, I caught three Northern pike. The average size was just over thirty-six inches. A fourth fish, reeled in almost to our boat, snapped my line like it was old thread. We both agreed, of course, that it was probably the biggest one by far. Forty-four inches at least. It grew to fifty inches by the time I got home.

the facilities

Minor Bay Lodge is the flagship property of Great White North Wilderness Resorts. Since the purchase of this resort the company has, every year, continued to improve the facilities. From renovating cabins to building new ones, to constantly upgrading boats and motors, and even placing picnic tables at their shore lunch sites, their goal is simply to make your stay as enjoyable as possible.

The lodge, built using pine trees from the surrounding forest, is comfortable and large enough to easily accommodate a full house of twenty-six guests. The season runs from early June through late August. During peak times, the staff count runs at twenty-three. They feel that this staff-to-guest ratio is necessary to maintain their standards of service.

Cabins range in size from two bedrooms to four bedrooms, accommodating from two up to eight people. Each offers all the comforts of home, plus great scenic vistas of the surrounding wilderness. Recent additions include two beautiful lakefront cabins. These lodgings feature knotty pine construction, four bedrooms, three bathrooms, two couches, six-foot dining table with matching coffee table, carpeting, lighted ceiling fans and designer picture windows offering great views of Wollaston Lake. One cabin even has a built-in sauna; the other offers a Jacuzzi tub. Rustic wood-framed cabins have been built at the exclusive outpost lakes. Each of these comes with propane stove, refrigerator, cooking utensils, bunk beds, lights, heater and propane barbecue. It gives a whole new meaning to the term "roughing it."

The boats available to all fishermen are custom designed eighteen- and twenty-footers, with swivel seats, floorboards, large casting decks, fish locators, trolling motors and quiet, non-polluting fifty-horsepower, four-stroke outboards.

leisure pursuits

The proprietors also operate another lodge, Slippery Winds Wilderness Resort, accessible only by boat or plane. When Duvell and his partner first saw the place in 1999, they were struck by its natural beauty and decided to add it to their growing family of fishing lodges.

The number of guests at Slippery Winds is limited to only sixteen, so the fishing pressure on these lakes has been greatly reduced. This fact, along with a long-standing catch and release program guarantees guests a phenomenal fishing experience. Last season, a number of notable fish were caught, including some great large-mouth and small-mouth bass, and a muskie measuring slightly over fifty inches.

The challenge each day is to decide which lake to fish. Three of the walk-in lakes are no more than an easy fifteen minute hike from one to the other, so all you need to bring are your rods and tackle. Each of the five main lakes average six to nine miles long, and are navigated easily with maps provided by the lodge. Your hosts keep abreast of all the hot spots and mark them accordingly.

Although it has only been a few years since the resort was taken over by Great White North, Slippery Winds Wilderness Lodge enjoys a core repeat clientele. This is always a key indicator as to the quality of experience offered.

the cuisine

Breakfast is served at 7:00 am sharp. It is usually made to order, and includes selections like omelets, fried or poached eggs, bacon, sausage, hash browns, and thick homemade toast. Fresh fruits and juices, coffee and hot chocolate accompany this hearty fare. At midday, you choose either a shore lunch of freshly caught fish or a packed lunch prepared by the kitchen.

Chef Loretta Maurice always makes dinner a memorable affair. On my second evening here, we began with a carrot, leek and celery soup served with bread right out of the oven. Our main course was chicken breast stuffed with spinach, mushrooms, green onions, carrots, zucchini and garlic. This was served on a bed of wild rice with thinly sliced carrots and beans al dente. For dessert, she brought us a red, white and blue pie. This beautifully layered presentation was made with raspberries, cheese cake and blueberries.

guest comments

"Just a short note to thank you for the wonderful experience I had as a guest of the Minor Bay Lodge. I can't say enough about the staff and how gracious they were to us on our recent stay. The weather cooperated and just added to the enjoyment that we had in catching the trophy fish, which we logged into the book every evening. I can't say enough about the guides and how helpful they were…all in all it was a wonderful experience and I highly recommend the Minor Bay Lodge to anyone who asks."

— *Frederic G. Novy, Chairman of the Board,*
Southwest Development Corporation

"Having returned from our third trip to Minor Bay Lodge, I wanted to write a note of appreciation to you for another fantastic trip to Wollaston Lake. Your staff continues to spoil our group with your great accommodations, excellent meals and terrific pike fishing. Finally, I want to compliment you on your guides Bob and Roland. Both of these men are truly professional and they make each day a unique experience filled with high expectations. Thanks for a great time!"

— *Dave Burba, Mid America Bank*

directions

Guests first fly to Saskatoon, Saskatchewan. This city is serviced by Northwest and United Airlines/Air Canada. The charter flight (Sunday and Thursday mornings) will then take you directly to their resort. For more information on this and their other properties, visit their website at —www.greatwhitenorthresorts.com.

REDOUBT MOUNTAIN LODGE

the place

In the year 2000, Eric and Shan Johnson joined in a partnership to create the Redoubt Mountain Lodge, deep in the Alaskan wilderness. Development of this area had begun forty years earlier when, in 1960, five acres were deeded to a Homer, Alaska family who built the original log cabin. In 1980, the land surrounding the site was designated Lake Clark National Park by then President Jimmy Carter.

The resort is located on beautiful Crescent Lake in the Chigmit Mountains of the Northern Aleutian Range. Crescent Lake is on the west side of salmon-rich Cook Inlet. The scenery is close to unbelievable, as Redoubt volcano, hanging glaciers and waterfalls greet the guests as they ready for the day's adventure.

I arrived here, as everybody does, by floatplane. It is an unforgettable trip. About an hour out of Anchorage as you begin to bank right, an awesome sight stretches out before you - towering mountains surrounding a lake of pure turquoise. This is where the lodge sits.

the people

The Johnson family has been involved in the fishing resort industry for over twenty years. Their first operation, on the Yentna River system in south central Alaska, is called Northwoods Lodge. This popular fishing lodge has been open since 1983. It is a remote resort accessible only by sea or air. Although only seventy-five miles northwest of Anchorage as the crow flies, it feels like a hundred years and many miles from civilization as we know it.

Back in 1972, Eric came to the Redoubt Mountain area while guiding a bear hunt. On his return home, he told Shan that it was the most beautiful place in Alaska that he had ever seen. It was a qualified opinion as he was born and raised in this state. In 1999, while surfing the internet, Shan came across a property for sale — The Redoubt Mountain Lodge. They became the new owners without hesitation.

the fishing

The lodge is located twenty river miles from Cook Inlet. This inlet boasts incredible runs of Sockeye and Coho salmon. Lake trout and large Arctic char are also fished throughout the season. Peak fishing season for most species of salmon is early July to mid-August. Coho are caught from August through October. When they start their run, it is not uncommon for anglers to catch twenty or more in a single day. While they practice catch-and-release on Arctic char and Lake trout, you are encouraged to take home your legal limit of salmon.

Whether fishing the long lake fork of the Crescent River, trolling for trout and char, fishing from the lodge's beach or boating the inlet's

waterways, a diverse and unique experience is yours for the taking. Huge Alaska King salmon and Lake trout topping the scales at twenty-five pounds are a common experience. During my visit, one of the guests hauled in a monster King weighing fifty-six pounds.

Redoubt has a fleet of eight boats and two ocean kayaks. Guests are accompanied by expert guides who are coast guard licensed and knowledgeable in all fishing techniques. All the gear you'll need — top line rods, reels, tackle and hip boots — is provided by the lodge.

the facilities

Redoubt's main lodge and five guest lodges can accommodate up to ten visitors at a time. Talk about remote — you would have to travel more than twenty-five miles in any direction to reach the next private acreage. The rest is all government-owned wilderness.

The main lodge is a cozy and comfortable custom-built structure that is framed with whole log spruce. The interior features thick carpeting and low-beamed ceilings. They have tastefully used exotic woods from Brazil — two dining room tables made of jatoba, and a floor surrounding the cone fireplace made of solid purple heart.

Each guest cabin is log, with a full-size and a twin-size bed, and a private bath. They even have a hand-built hot tub. It sits in a beautiful wood-and-glass gazebo that offers a spectacular 180-degree view of the lake and mountains.

Alaskan Brown bear come in droves to Crescent Lake to fish for the Sockeye salmon. They remain through the fall, with September seeing the largest numbers. The parkland surrounding the lodge is also home to black bear, moose, wolves, otter, beaver, mink and marten. Add the scenic mountain backdrop, and you are guaranteed some amazing photo opportunities. This area is for the real outdoor enthusiast. The more hardy souls can be found hiking on a glacier or kayaking in the sea.

the cuisine

Three buffet-style meals are served daily in the lodge dining room. The chef at Redoubt Mountain prepares sumptuous Alaskan dishes like Sugar Spiced Salmon, Marinated Orange Salmon, Halibut and Alaskan King Crab. Other fare might include pork chops with coconut rum and caramelized pineapple sauce.

Dinner on the evening of my stay began with a grilled flatbread served with an artichoke, garlic and parmesan cheese dip. Then came their Caesar Salad, followed by a rosemary and garlic dijon chicken with grilled zucchini. Dessert was a homemade strawberry-wild rhubarb crumble, made from the local harvest.

a day in the life of...the vanderzanden family

Tom and Jonnie VanderZanden, along with their son, Jesse and his wife Amy arrived three days before I got here. As a group, they would rise sometime after 7:00 am and meet for breakfast. After organizing the day's gear, including a packed lunch, all would be on the water fishing by 9:30 am. They would get so caught up in their angling pursuits that, on average, nine hours would pass before returning to the lodge.

After enjoying a few drinks and a fine dinner, they would meet with owners Eric and Shan to discuss fishing and their other passion — the Alaska Outdoor Council. Son Jesse works for this organization, whose prime mandate is to look out for the interests of the Alaskan sportsman. Depending on the intensity of the conversation, the day would end sometime between 10:00 pm and midnight.

guest comments

"Thanks for running a first-class operation."

— *Jim Fabro, Pearl River, New York*

"As always, an absolutely wonderful time with fantastic fishing, food and company. Thank you all very much, see you soon."

— *Shawn Bohannan, Snohomish, Washington*

"Wonderful time! Beautiful area…and six silvers on the fly…the Best!"

— *Greg Gorgas, September, 2001*

directions

Redoubt Mountain Lodge is located fifty miles west of Kenai and 100 miles southwest of Anchorage, Alaska. Guests book flights from home to either Anchorage or Kenai. A professional air taxi company will then fly you directly to the lodge. Flight times range from forty-five to seventy minutes. For more information, visit their website at — www.redoubtmountainlodge.com.

RUBY SPRINGS LODGE

the place

It has been said that fly fishing in the Rocky Mountains is more than a sum of its parts. Sure, pristine rivers offer a place for trout to grow up wild, which is hard to find anymore. And fly fishermen come here for the mountains too, and the solitude, and for the small town atmosphere.

But for some, there is one last ingredient that's critical to the ultimate Montana angling experience — a great home base. It is these people who have found Ruby Springs Lodge. It sits on a beautiful spread of land 5,100 feet above sea level, near the town of Alder in southwest Montana. It is a full-service destination fly fishing resort set right on the banks of the Ruby River.

Meandering through the valley that bears its name, the Ruby River flows through the Tobacco Root and Ruby Mountain Ranges. It is considered by many to be one of the premiere dry fly fisheries in the Rockies. Ruby Springs visitors — a maximum of only twelve at any one time — are privileged to have over ten miles of privately leased water on three different ranches in the most productive stretches of the river.

In an article for *Town & Country* magazine, writer Charles Gaines summed it up like this:

> *"I wrote in an article that I believed they would, in very short order, make Ruby Springs one of the four or five best of the relatively new breed of small lodges in the Rockies that specialize in fly fishing for trout, yet offer other diversions for the non-fisher as well, along with such emollients for all as a chef from the Seattle Culinary Institute and posh cabins featuring heated bathrooms with heated floor tiles and twelve-inch shower heads. I was wrong on two counts — they did it immediately upon opening their doors, and the place has fewer, if any, peers."*

the people

Open since 1994, Ruby Springs Lodge was built by John and Krista Sampson, and Paul and Jeanne Moseley. Best friends since grade school, John and Paul spent their first few years in the region as fishing guides, learning everything from what clients wanted and needed, to where the most consistent fishing could be found. It was that experience that led them to the Ruby Valley, and the establishment of this great resort.

In fact, both John and Paul still guide some of their guests. John's wife Krista has done some guiding as well, and together with Paul's wife Jeanne, they assist in the management of all lodge staff. John points out that everyone helps to walk that fine line between treating guests like old friends and new royalty. It is a balance they have mastered.

the fishing

The Ruby River conveniently flows withing casting range of the dining room. Three stretches offer a range of different cover, from angler-friendly to ultra-challenging. On any section you are apt to find hatches of pale morning duns in June and July, caddis throughout the summer and baetis hatches in the fall. Late in the season you can also enjoy what some say is the best warm-weather grasshopper fishing in Montana.

After fishing the Ruby for a few days, some of the guests wanted to fish new waters. They teamed up with their guides to float through the scenic canyons or along the pastures of the Big Hole, Beaverhead, Jefferson or Madison Rivers. In all, there are five blue ribbon trout streams within easy striking distance from the lodge.

The Beaverhead is one of the best trophy trout streams in southwestern Montana, harboring a population of 3,800 fish per mile

that average seventeen inches. This river offers any angler an honest shot at landing a wild trout of twenty-plus inches.

The river that many believe is what a trout river should look like is the Big Hole. Dry fly fishing here kicks off with the June emergence of the salmonfly. With its fishing, scenery and perfect riffles, the Big Hole is a true classic.

The Madison River is still one of the most consistently good fisheries in the state. Caddis, mayflies, hoppers and salmonflies entice browns and rainbows to the surface all year long. And then there's the Jefferson River. Despite contending with low flows due to heavy summer irrigation, the Jefferson can quietly be one of the best rivers in the state at certain times of year. And you may even have it all to yourself.

the facilities

Ruby Springs is a resort designed for fly fishermen by fly fishermen. It sits on stunning 700-acre ranch, overlooking five miles of private river and a spring-fed pond. All is, of course, surrounded by mountains and the expanse of a Montana sky.

Within minutes of my arrival, I was given the grand tour by Molly Rawn. The lodge and its six individual cabins are nestled among the cottonwoods of the Ruby River. All the cabins have been created to deliver everything you need, with king or twin beds in an open floor plan, river rock fireplaces, screened porches, heated tile floors and oversized showers. The total effect is maximum comfort.

The recommended stop before dinner is the River Room, a log-appointed "mini" lodge with a central stone fireplace. It is where everyone gathers to have a drink, trade fish stories and sample some incredible appetizers.

The main lodge affords great views from its spacious salon, fly tying room, library and dining room. The architecture only adds to its airy, rustic feel, from the open ceiling and rafters to the stone fireplace. During my stay I found that most guests, after a long day on the water, enjoyed spending their evenings right here.

leisure pursuits

Due to the amazing fact that some people don't want to fish every day all day, Ruby Springs has provided some great alternatives. Some of the more popular activities include horseback rides in the surrounding mountain ranges, hiking, and day trips to the historic gold mining towns of Virginia City and Nevada City. Good golf can be found nearby at Madison Meadows in Ennis or the Old Works Course up in Anaconda. For those who want to sharpen their skills with a shotgun, they have a regulation skeet range on the property.

the cuisine

As with many of the new generation of fishing resorts, particular attention is paid to the food and wine lists. Gone are the old days when the food was simply "hearty fare." Today's sophisticated angler requires and is given much more. To accomplish this they employ the talents of Executive Chef Micko Reijo and his wife Gay. Micko hails from Sweden, and from a family of chefs going back generations.

All guests start the day off with beverages delivered to the door of their cabin. Next, a plentiful breakfast in the main lodge featuring pancakes or French toast topped with fresh berries, or perhaps scrambled eggs with smoked salmon and chives.

When I sat down to dinner, I was amazed to find that there were four entrées to choose from. We began with an Organic Spinach and Frisse Salad tossed with pistachio oil and 20-year-old balsamic vinegar and accompanied by portobello mushrooms, figs, and Italian hard goat cheese. I decided on the homemade

ravioli for the main course. It came stuffed with fennel and leeks served with a light tomato saffron sauce and accompanied by sauteed Alaskan spot prawns. Dessert later appeared in the form of a Bavarian chocolate tort served with raspberry coulis.

a day in the life of…tom depping

Hailing from Kingwood, Texas and Breckinridge, Colorado, Tom began coming here the year they opened. He has never missed a year since. My timing for an interview was perfect. I sat down with him on the evening of the best day of trout fishing that he had ever had.

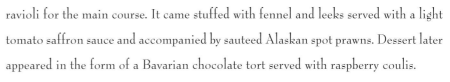
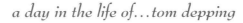

Usually up around 7:00 am, he has some of the coffee and juice that has been delivered to his cabin door. After enjoying a substantial breakfast, he meets up with

his guide. They then head out to the chosen fishing spot for the day. His first line is in the water by 9:30 am. Approaching one o'clock, they will take a break and enjoy a shore lunch.

When the fishing day is done, its back to the lodge. It will be sometime between 6:00 and 7:00 pm, depending on their location and the response of the fish. Then back to the cabin to freshen up and join the other fishermen at the cocktail party. After trading fish tales, they all sit down to another gourmet meal. After dinner, Tom and the other guests will sit around the fireplace on the outdoor porch and discuss everything from world events to the next day's fishing locations.

guest comments

"Crown jewel of southwestern Montana. Food, service, and guides were super. Facilities are five-star. Thanks for the experience."

— *Wayne H., Shreveport, Louisiana*

"The beauty of the accommodations matched the loveliness of this gem of a valley. The graciousness of the staff is unflagging — must be something in the Montana water! Speaking of which, the fishing was great, thanks to our guide's patience and expertise."

— *Ned and Nancy F., Seattle, Washington*

"We had a wonderful time. The food, fishing and staff are terrific. See you next year."

— *Bob and Michelle D., New York, New York*

"Instant relaxation the moment we arrived. We are leaving five pounds heavier than when we arrived. Thanks to our guides for all our wonderful fishing. We caught two big ones. Mine was at least 20 pounds! Remember women, don't lie about the size. What a wonderful experience. Thanks to all the staff."

— Bill And Jane K., Portland, Oregon

directions

Most guests choose to fly to Butte, Montana, and then drive to the lodge. From the airport, turn onto Hwy. 2, and drive 21 miles to Hwy. 41. Go left, travel 12 miles to the "T" in the road, and turn right onto Hwy. 55. Go straight through past Sheridan to Laurin. The lodge is 1/3 mile past Laurin on the right. For more information visit their website at — www.rubyspringslodge.com.

SELWYN LAKE LODGE

the place

Way back in the year 1770, Samuel Hearne was the first person of European descent to encounter Selwyn Lake in the very northern end of Saskatchewan. He was on a mission seeking yellow copper for his employer, the Hudson Bay Company. He didn't stay.

For the next 200 years, the only people to fish this remote lake were the native Indian tribes, managing the resources responsibly as their ancestors had done for thousands of years.

Enter Gordon Wallace and family. He was a bush pilot and outdoorsman who had been hunting high and low for a place to build their dream — a large and remote fishing resort accessible only by air. After hunting and fishing Selwyn Lake for a number of years, he recognized that their dream could be realized right here, on this very lake.

Located in a spot where lakes and rivers flow together to form the vast Arctic Watershed, Selwyn Lake is indeed remote, located more than 800 miles from Winnipeg, Manitoba and 650 miles from Saskatoon, Saskatchewan. It crosses Canada's 60th parallel into the remote Northwest Territories. In fact, a third of the lake is in Saskatchewan, with the balance in the Northwest Territories.

There are literally hundreds of islands on Selwyn Lake, all covered with birch, jackpine, tamarack and black spruce trees. With ax in hand, Wallace and a few hardy friends began hewing the landscape. Materials were flown in on a float-equipped C-47 cargo plane. It took no less than twenty-seven flights to bring all the needed materials to the site.

Wildlife abounds here, including bear, moose, caribou, lynx, wolverine, geese and the famous Bald eagle. In these surroundings, amidst sand eskers, peat moss beds, rocky ridges and permafrost sits the Selwyn Lake Lodge, offering up some of Canada's finest fishing opportunities.

the people

Gordon and Mary Daigneault-Wallace are your hosts. They have been a part of the north for decades. Gord was an aviator in these parts and Mary was a Northern outpost medical nurse. The pair met while flying medical air evacuations. Mary, of native Cree and French ancestry, was raised on the land in the traditional lifestyle of the Metis people.

With the sale of their northern air service in 1991, they decided to develop Selwyn Lake, the last major fishery available, into one of North America's finest upscale trophy lodges. Since opening in 1993, they have been here for their guests every day, and are quite proud to report that the majority of these guests are repeat bookings.

Their partners, Jim Yuel of PIC Group and his son, Greg, take an active role in ensuring that this resort continues its tradition of being one of the finest tourist and fishing destinations in the world. Their involvement came as a result of Jim's love of fishing. He has been an avid sportsman, hunting and fishing Canada for decades. Over the years, his dream of becoming part of a first class fishing lodge grew. In 1996, during a trip to Selwyn Lake Lodge as a guest, he found what he was looking for — a luxurious lodge in a pristine setting on a remote body of water.

the fishing

Real Canadian wilderness greeted our group of fourteen as we flew in on the float plane. The lake is immense, stretching forty-five miles from end to end, and eighteen miles across — some 135,000 acres of water. With all the islands, bays and marshes, the number of trophy fishing holes is beyond comprehension.

Selwyn Lake is fed by numerous streams, with two outflowing rivers that flow into the Athabasca drainage system and ultimately to the Arctic Ocean. Although never surveyed, depths have been reported to 300 feet. The bottom is just as rugged as the surrounding area, with many shallow reefs. The water is so pure and clear that a fishing lure can be seen flashing as deep as thirty feet.

The fishing at this resort can only be described as outstanding — anglers will find no better catch-to-cast ratio anywhere. The lake boasts some of the largest populations of Arctic grayling, Northern pike and Lake trout. Fly-fishing for pike here can be a life-changing event, with twenty to thirty pounders a common occurrence. Don Lamont, host of The Complete Angler television show, recently caught seven trout in one session, all over twenty-four pounds!

Trained and certified professional guides are included in your vacation and ensure your angling experience is both productive and relaxing. Continuous training each year maintains guide accreditation and results in a dynamic group of seasoned staff. The lodge employs local guides from northern Saskatchewan who are familiar with the best fishing spots.

My guide for the day was Stan Clarke, a friend of Gord's and retired RCMP officer who avidly pursues his depth of knowledge and understanding about fly fishing, along with new lake fishing techniques. Twenty minutes into our fishing trip, I hooked my first ever Northern pike. Stan told me it looked like a "fair fish." Right. When landed, it tipped the scales at fifteen pounds and measured thirty-six inches. To me, it was a monster! Back at the lodge I soon discovered that he was right. My fish was, indeed, only a fair size. At least a dozen Northerns were caught that outweighed mine. The record for the day, duly noted on the "bragging board", was a leviathan weighing over thirty pounds and measuring two inches shy of four feet.

the facilities

A hand-cut log boardwalk leads you from the dock up to the lodge. Inside, the guest rooms are spacious, each with twin beds and a private bath. The suites are connected by a wrap-around deck which extends along to the dining room. A recent addition is the "Honeymoon/Executive" Suite, where you can enjoy the ultimate in luxury and privacy.

Inside the lodge you will find a dining room, a fireside lounge surrounded by elegant and relaxing leather chairs, a games room and bar. It's the perfect setting for enjoying a cocktail while discussing the day' adventures. They make you feel right at home here. You can even raid the refrigerator in the middle of the night, if you have the energy to get out of bed.

It quickly becomes apparent that the staff of Selwyn Lake Lodge are committed to your individual attention. That is why they have kept it small, private and flexible to each guest's needs. The rooms, facilities, fishing equipment and boats are all state-of-the-art. A nice surprise given their remote location.

If their remoteness is not enough for you, they do offer an outpost camp. It is twenty-four miles north of the main lodge, yet still on Selwyn Lake. The wood cabin here comes complete with refrigerator, freezer, stove, running water, warm showers and all cooking utensils. Before you arrive they fully stock the fridge. The outpost features Lund boats equipped with fish finders, flat deck, swivel seats and environmentally-friendly Honda motors.

leisure pursuits

Selwyn Lake Lodge has gained a reputation as a top-notch bear and moose hunting destination. The unparalleled acreage and variety of habitat are the main reasons. But the luxury of the lodge coupled with the great hunting make this an sportsman's nirvana. The people here are proud to have achieved a 100% satisfaction rating from their bear hunting guests during the past three seasons.

The beautiful scenery is an attraction in and of itself. Add the occasional viewing of the spectacular Northern Lights. Then throw in the fishing and accommodations, and you will probably leave this place as I did — in a trance. One that wears off ever so slowly.

the cuisine

The food at this resort is world class, an oasis of civility in the northern wilderness. Travel magazine raves, "Breakfasts and dinners with fine wines and cocktails would challenge any five-star hotel in any city along the 49th parallel or below. And then there is the shore lunch of pan-fried freshly caught fish fillets. Always the highlight of the day."

Our day began at 7:00 am, when we all met for breakfast. Choices included Selwyn Lake waffles, French toast, pancakes and omelets, all served with bacon, sausage or ham. At noon, our guide put on his "chef hat" as we dined al fresco out on the lake. They prepare all meals, from baked fish to chowder, over an open flame. After setting foot back on dry land at the end of the day, hors d'oeuvres and beverages awaited us. These were followed by the evening's dining experience. We started with a salad of baby spinach greens topped with crisp bacon, crimini mushrooms, egg and Bermuda onion, all complimented with an Italian vinaigrette. The main course featured smoked peppered pork loin medallions over Saskatoon berry demi-glace, with duchess potatoes and a mosaic of fresh vegetables. For dessert, we had the chef's homemade vanilla ice cream presented with a banana rum sauce.

a day in the life of...the Lehman family

Jim Lehman first came to this lodge back in the mid-1990s. He returned this year with his father, Kieffer, and his son, Mike. The Lehman clan, all three generations of them, arrived here from Indiana for a four-day vacation. The day I interviewed them, they had just returned from a day of fishing. Their total catch was more than eighty Northern pike and twenty lake trout.

They awaken in order of their age, with Kieffer up first, followed by Jim and then, somewhat reluctantly, Mike. Then it's over to the dining room to join the rest of the guests for breakfast. After fortifying for the day, they meet up with their guide down at the dock, load up the boat and begin the next fishing adventure.

Returning to the lodge around 5:00 pm, it is time for a shower, change of clothes and back to the lodge for cocktails, appetizers and the four-course feast that will begin at 7:00 pm. After dinner there is more discussion on the day's fishing, and tomorrow's plan.

guest comments

"Twenty-six lake trout from twenty to thirty pounds, and all before lunch! There's one other thing that keeps me coming back to Selwyn — you can always get out fishing, even on the windiest days ... very few expanses of open water. Not the case with many other trout lakes."

— *Dick Sternberg, Director, The Hunting and Fishing Library*

"Thanks to you and thanks to your wonderful team for a vacation of a lifetime for our family The five of us came to Selwyn with a lot of enthusiasm and no fishing skills. We left feeling a little humble about the tremendous experience we were privileged to have."

— *Nick, Pam, Ben and Grant Horn*

"Thank you for ensuring your trip totally met and exceeded our expectations. The new lodge is a beautiful addition. Our guide made a real effort to guarantee we were where the big fish were biting."

— *Mike and Lynette Gilbertson, Northwestern Airlines*

directions

Selwyn Lake Lodge sits on Snowshoe Island just south of Canada's 60th parallel. Convenient flight connections to Saskatoon and a private charter to Selwyn Lake make this resort easily and quickly accessible from anywhere in North America. For more information, visit their website at — www.selwynlakelodge.com

SONORA RESORT

the place

On a small island amidst the stark beauty that is the Inside Passage of Vancouver Island, British Columbia sits the Sonora Resort. Visited by captains of industry, movie stars and angling enthusiasts from the world over, this lodge has earned a reputation for providing unparalleled luxury, fishing, gourmet cuisine and first-class adventure.

This place is truly a destination resort. Their three-acre property is home to the docks, main lodge, twenty-five rooms and suites and a 2,000-square-foot meeting facility. The property, with its outdoor heated pool, hot tubs, tennis court and helicopter landing pad, was carefully built to blend in beautifully with its natural surroundings.

I flew here from Vancouver with a group of new guests. After a short and scenic flight we landed and taxied up to the dock. We were met by several staff, including Mike Flint, the general manager. After being shown the lay of the land, I checked into my suite and then immediately joined the others to discuss the afternoon's fishing adventure.

the people

Twenty years ago, most fishing lodges offered the basic necessities that only the avid angler would find adequate. In the 1980's, Mike Gallant had a vision of creating a different kind of fishing destination. He built a resort on his property at Sonora Island. He wanted the new place to offer convenience of access, luxurious accommodations, gourmet fare, fine wines and fantastic fishing in an atmosphere of casual opulence. Over a period of fifteen years, he built Sonora Resort into a world-renowned fishing destination. In March of 2000, after achieving the lofty goals that he had set, he decided to retire to Vancouver Island. The current owners, The H.Y. Louie Group, continue to build on his vision.

Through a mutual acquaintance, Mike Flint met Mike Gallant and began his career at Sonora as an evening bartender. Flint, through diligence, hard work and commitment, worked his way to the top. His path included positions as Public Relations, Sales Associate, Operations Manager and in 2000, appointment to General Manager. His successful journey up the "corporate ladder" is a rare commodity in today's marketplace.

He now surrounds himself with a team that believes in this place, and treats the Sonora Resort like its their own home. He summed up his feelings when he told me, "What other lodge on the coast resides in the Beverly Hills of the Pacific Northwest?"

the fishing

Sonora is steeped in a rich tradition of fishing for big Chinook salmon. Once they hit thirty pounds and over, the world knows them as the famous Tyee. The other salmon in

great demand — and supply — is the Coho. Catching a twenty-five pound salmon at 120 feet down using a seven-pound test line is fishing at its absolute finest.

They have an expert guide and a twenty-four-foot Grady White for every two guests. Their guides are the cream of the crop — average professional experience is an amazing twenty years. Running the rapids from the dock out to Denham Bay, a popular spot for big fish, is a thrill in itself. Once there, the fishing is usually fantastic, as these monster fish stage awhile before running up or gliding down the rapids.

Another great fishing hole is called the Dump. So named because the restricted narrows here choke the tide and "dump" all kinds of good feed into the water. This spot becomes an angler's paradise every tide change, and is a perfect spot for buck tailing Coho.

Sonora also offers a world-class fly fishing program from March 15 through April 30th. You travel by helicopter or jet boat the glacier-fed river systems. These crystal-clear rivers offer up Dolly Varden, browns, steelhead and rainbow trout. Every cast is an angler's paradise.

the facilities

Sonora Resort offers a nice variety of classy and comfortable accommodations. Each of their luxury suites is uniquely constructed with guest rooms opening into a large common

area. Amenities differ, but in most you will find bedrooms with en suite and jacuzzis, rock fireplaces, steam rooms and hot tubs. These suites also feature vaulted ceilings and huge picture windows offering vistas of the wilderness outside.

All rooms are connected by a wooden walkway to the main lodge and dining room. This is the center of activity. When not fishing, guests go from here to the outdoor swimming pool, lap pool, fitness center, or volleyball and tennis courts. For those into maximum comfort, they also have four steam rooms, and a Relaxation Centre with a variety of spa treatments available from their two resident massage therapists. There is also a games room in the lodge complete with an antique English snooker table. This beauty spans six-by-twelve feet — a real challenge for visitors used to playing on the smaller five-by-ten American tables.

leisure pursuits

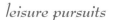

Many view this resort as not just a fishing lodge, but a wilderness retreat. There are many ways to get out into the untouched beauty of coastal British Columbia. Those inclined can go hiking through the flora and fauna of Sonora Island, while keeping an eye out for the elusive grizzly or majestic bald eagle.

Sonora also offers helicopter excursions up to massive glaciers, or a Zodiac trip in search of orca whales and dolphins found in these waters. Some choose to get close-up and personal with the coastline in an ocean kayak. Other pleasurable pursuits include whitewater rafting in the Southgate River and going to the grizzly bear Watching Towers at the Orford River. Whatever your outdoor pleasure, you will probably find it here.

the cuisine

The food served - breakfast, lunch and dinner — is all gourmet class and is served in a variety of interesting venues. Everything from deluxe picnic lunches for days of adventure to evening feasts on the catch of the day.

Breakfast is a hearty sit-down affair with such delectable dishes as eggs florentine and huevos rancheros. They also, of course, serve up all the standards - bacon, ham, sausage, pancakes and eggs along with fresh fruits and breads. Lunches here are unique. Sometime near noon, as the fishermen are starting to get hungry, the "Chuckwagon" appears on the water. It is a converted aluminum fishing boat that has three barbecues on the stern and delivers hot gourmet lunches to each of the resort's boats.

The dinners usually have a theme, and an entire meal can have an Asian or a Moroccan flair. On the evening of my visit, we were served what has become the resort's signature dish. It is called Sonora Salmon. A freshly caught salmon is marinated in, among other things, rye whisky and an Indonesian condiment called ketjap manis (like soy sauce, except richer and sweeter). Then, after a brief grilling on the barbecue, it is placed on parchment paper and baked in the oven. It is out of this world.

guest comments

"Just a note to thank you for your hospitality. You have the best fishing lodge I have ever been to. The attention to detail, the staff, your wine cellar is without compare. To say nothing of your masseuse....the best who has ever worked on me."

— *Larry Hagman, Beverly Hills, California*

"We have been to many places throughout the world during our travels, and your service, employee enthusiasm, professionalism and charisma far exceeds most of these places. Your kindness and thoughtfulness were greatly appreciated…you should be exceedingly proud of your performance."

— *Dr. C.E. McCoy, Dallas, Texas*

"Awesome! Awesome! Awesome! We just loved it. Great staff, eagles, bears, dolphins and a 23-pound beautiful salmon. God's paradise, we will be back."

— *Jack & Maureen Wilson, Vancouver, British Columbia*

Most hospitality services meet the expectations of their customers. You, however, exceeded expectations and delighted us beyond our imaginations. Very fine food and very friendly and considerate staff."

— *Hiram Chen, Toronto, Ontario*

directions

Guests of the resort travel to Vancouver International Airport in British Columbia. From here a private charter aircraft will take you over fifty-five minutes of spectacular scenery and land you at the resort's dock. For more information visit their website at — www.sonoraresort.com.

SPOTTED BEAR RANCH

the place

The South Fork of Montana's Flathead River is one of the last fisheries in this state where you can still find only native fish. While plenty of rivers have outstanding fishing for imported brown or rainbow trout, only the South Fork has native Westslope cutthroats and bull trout. And to fish for Westslope cutts is to experience Montana fishing as it truly was a century ago, before man impacted the fisheries. The tale of this cutthroat parallels that of the eastern brook trout. Both require exceptionally clean, cold water. And since both strike aggressively, it is easy to over harvest.

But here, these cutthroats flourish, and for two reasons. First, the river flows through remote country, the Bob Marshall Wilderness. Second, stringent management policies have been in place since 1982. Since those regulations were implemented, catches have tripled and average fish size has shot up more than two inches.

Originating at the confluence of Youngs and Danaher Creeks, the South Fork flows north, ironically, for forty-five miles before emptying into Hungry Horse Reservoir. Primitive and cobbled with smooth multi-colored rocks shaped by eons of fast-moving water, the South Fork of the Flathead River is indeed a most unique spot for fishing. It offers sensational dry-fly fishing, spectacular scenery, and most surprising of all, solitude.

Most of this wilderness area is accessible only by foot or horseback, and thus remains truly wild and unspoiled. In reality, the majority of the few that fish these waters are backpackers, working their way through the forested lands heading for Gordon's Pass or some other vantage point from which to enjoy the surrounding vistas.

Even more appealing for the angler and sportsman is Spotted Bear Ranch. It is the only lodge on the South Fork. Access to this place is by way of a fifty-mile unpaved road. If you choose to drive here as most do, travel this section carefully — there is wildlife everywhere. During my two-hour trip, I saw a total of seven whitetail deer, four elk, two rabbits and an incredible golden eagle, all on or beside the road. Although Spotted Bear has been operating as a guest ranch for more than half a century, it has been called "Montana's best kept secret." Not any more.

the people

Kirk Gentry owned a sports marketing business for many years. But he wasn't content with what he had. So he made a list of his passions, and two of these ranked high - fly fishing and horseback riding. With that in mind he began his quest. It ended when he found and bought the Spotted Bear Ranch. He is now living his dream.

His right-hand man is Fred Haney. Originally from Indiana, he left the field of engineering to pursue what he loved best — fishing. After guiding in Colorado and Argentina, he settled in Montana. In 1994, he met Kirk, and after several meetings, began guiding at the Ranch. He is now their general manager.

the fishing

On water inaccessible to most, the staff of the Spotted Bear put me and a few fellow guests onto stretches of river that most fishermen only dream of. The river is so secluded, the fishing pressure so light, and fishery management policies so progressive, it is not uncommon to catch twenty-five to thirty fish in a single day.

The guests have their choice of fishing expeditions — lodge-based trips, float and wade fishing in fourteen-foot inflatable boats, hike and wade fishing the smaller waters, or float fishing the mountain lakes.

For the serious outdoorsman, there is the Wilderness Pack and Float Expedition. This is a combination of riding, camping, floating and fishing through the Bob Marshall Wilderness for the first two days. The third day is a layover, and guests hike to fish waters near the camp. The fourth and fifth days are spent floating and wade fishing their way down the South Fork to the take out point. Every trip includes an experienced, professional guide. In fact, Spotted Bear has one for every two guests. Because of the exclusivity and quality of fishing, this option has become the most popular trip. Testament to this fact is the award they received, the 2001 *Orvis-endorsed Expedition of The Year."*

Fishing for the Westslope cutthroat is a memorable experience. They are not finicky eaters. One guide described it to me as "ten years fishing in a five-day trip." These firm bodied fighters range in size from eight to twenty inches. Bull trout, although approaching double-digit weights, are protected and if caught, must be released immediately. And while Westslope cutts are not picky about what they bite, they are very hard to spot. With silver sides and olive backs, they tend to hold in broken water over the many-colored stones that serve as perfect camouflage.

Although there are bag and size limits designed to protect mature fish and provide backpackers with a nice lunch at the same time, out here catch and release is the name of the game.

the facilities

Guests of the lodge stay in one of four two-bedroom cabins. While rustic on the outside, the inside of these cabins provides all the comforts of home, with private baths, carpeted floors and wood-burning fireplaces.

The historic main lodge is a warm and inviting place. It is poised on a bluff overlooking the South Fork. The interior decor is wonderful, with a sunken living room surrounding a huge log firepit, and plenty of comfortable club chairs for lounging. Trophy fish, elk and deer adorn most walls and an antique piano sits in the corner. Huge picture windows offer panoramic views of the river and forest beyond.

The lodge supplies almost everything. You can bring your favorite rod and reel, or get one from the Orvis-endorsed Shop, which also features flies, other fishing equipment and some unique novelties.

The sense of a real wilderness adventure hit me when I realized that there is absolutely no connection to the outside world. There are no telephones, no cell phone reception, no faxes and no television. Wonderful.

leisure pursuits

From late October through to the end of November, it is deer season at the Spotted Bear Ranch. Large populations of whitetail and mule deer inhabit the area surrounding the lodge. A significant elk population also resides here, and many guests choose to combine a deer hunt with an elk hunt. Generally, you will hunt within a ten-to-fifteen mile radius of the lodge. Usually, the hunt involves a drive to an area, then a two mile hike to reach the best spots. There have, however, been trophy bucks taken within two miles of the lodge. The success rate here has been historically high.

Black bear hunts are another diversion, with three Spring hunts open to a maximum of six guests each. The lodge serves as base camp; the tracking done in four-by-four vehicles or on foot. At this time of year, these bears are newly emerged from hibernation, and the sleek, fresh coats of brown, cinnamon, blonde or black make magnificent trophies.

For the more genteel set, backpacking and camping opportunities abound. The ranch is located about sixty miles from Glacier National Park. That, in itself, deserves at least half a day, if not more.

the cuisine

Breakfast and dinner are served in the main lodge dining room. Lunches are served on the shore of the river, as you take a well-deserved break from the fishing. Hors d'oeuvres appear nightly around six o'clock, with a hearty home-style supper served an hour or so later. The staff deliver fresh beverages to your room in the morning, and will even light the fire in the cabin's fireplace to get you started.

Dinner on the evening of my visit began around 7:00 pm with appetizers, the tastiest of which were the crab-stuffed mushrooms wrapped in bacon and barbecued. We started off our main meal with their House Specialty salad - spinach, water chestnuts, bacon and a secret homemade sauce. The entree followed, featuring char-broiled prime cut steak served with baked potato, fresh green beans and corn. Dessert was a choice of huckleberry cheesecake or German chocolate cake.

a day in the life of...the martinek family

Dennis and Suzie Martinek, along with their son Mark decided to try fly fishing for the first time in their lives. So they booked a vacation, left their home in Fallbrook, California and drove here.

On their first morning, after breakfast, they sat down with the guides for an instructive introduction to fly fishing. Around 9:30 am, it was time to go fishing. At 11:00 o'clock, after putting on waders, they began to fish Spotted Bear Lake. The first time they put their rods in the water, all three of them caught fish! The feisty Arctic grayling were biting like crazy. Average catch was in the sixteen inch range. Later in the day they also began to catch some Westslope cutthroats.

The fishing was so spectacular that they didn't get back to the lodge until after 7:00 pm. Then it was time to quickly freshen up and join the other guests for the evening meal. At 10:30 that night, all three of them

were still with the guides working on the fine art of fly tying. A new family of fly fishing enthusiasts was born that day.

guest comments

"Yes — dreams do come true! The best fishing my buddy, John and I have had in 35 years."

— *Rich von Lossberg, La Crescenta, California*

"I've been to Paris and Cancun. I've seen the Grand Canyon and Yellowstone Park. But I've never been anywhere that I enjoyed as much as the Spotted Bear Ranch. It was an experience that will cause other vacations to fade from memory. I truly enjoyed the company and advice of our guide, Doug. He almost embarrassed me with his attentiveness and respect. He alone is a treasure. I can't wait to get back."

— *Dick Melstrom, Cadillac, Michigan*

"I have just had a week to reflect on the magnificent trip my son and I had at Spotted Bear Ranch. My son not only learned how to fly fish, he caught more fish than me! Our guide, Andy, made our adventure one that we'll never forget."

— *Steve Turner, Chicago, Illinois*

directions

Their lodge sits in northwest Montana. Their operations are based in Kalispell, with the actual facilities located in the Flathead National Forest. The drive will take you from two to three hours. For detailed directions, visit their website at — www.spottedbear.com.

THE SPOTTED HORSE RANCH

the place

Homesteaded more than a century ago, the land south of Jackson Hole, Wyoming in the Teton National Forest has been home to trappers, settlers, farmers and cowboys. The valley that cradles the Hoback River has been cultivated by working ranchers for generations.

As times changed, simple one-room log homes and rustic cabins gave way to guest ranches for the "dudes" that came in from the cities, looking to live the dream of the free and open American West. Fresh air, unspoiled natural surroundings and the feeling that time forgot to move this area along were in great demand. And still are to this day.

Amidst all this, at an elevation of 6,400 feet, is the Spotted Horse Ranch. Beginning life as a hunting camp more than 100 years ago, it has retained much of that feel today. It has deep roots and is characteristic of the way the West looked ages ago. The Spotted Horse is what the old West was all about. It is an outpost of casual comfort in the center of spectacular mountain country.

In the valley created by four mountain ranges, the runoff from nearly 400 inches of snow each year provides the region with some of the best streams and rivers for spawning and growing trout, including the Snake River fine-spotted cutthroat. Rainbows and browns also thrive in some of these waters. Active and hungry, these fish gobble up flies and will fight hard for their prize when hooked.

This historic and beautiful area provides the perfect backdrop for an unforgettable fishing adventure.

the people

When Tony Royal and Sam Blount started visiting the west in the 1980's, they always talked about finding "a small place." Each had successful careers in the corporate world back in the southeast, but as many have found, starting with Lewis and Clark, the West holds a certain powerful allure. The Rocky Mountain "bug" bit Sam in his younger days when he was a river guide on the Colorado River.

The vision of a small ranch with good trout fishing, good water, beautiful scenery and horses would be achieved with the renovation of the Spotted Horse Ranch. This place had been listed in previous publications, but Tony and Sam brought in Orvis to endorse their new destination and focus more on fly fishing, guiding, schools and classes.

The Jackson Hole Trout School was established, with Dave Wickline as chief instructor. Dave has fished and guided in the Jackson Hole area for close to a decade, managing Orvis-endorsed outfitting and guide services. He caught his first trout at age seven, and has never looked back.

Patty Reilly has been guiding and instructing in and around this area for more than twenty years. Her wealth of experience includes guiding in Argentina. She has instructed around the country, and works well with both men and women fly-fishers.

Tony Royal is the host, ranch owner and resident jack-of-all-trades. He started an outfitting service in South Carolina called Bay Street Outfitters, and offers instruction on both fresh and salt water, having fished the Rockies for more than twenty years. Simply put, the Spotted Horse Ranch is a lifelong dream come true for Sam and Tony.

the fishing

When Tony and Sam took over this place, they immediately added to and put more emphasis on fly fishing, thus the Orvis presence and the Trout School. Their school focuses on the beginner to intermediate skilled fisherman. It involves two days of classroom instruction, and one day of guided fishing, where students implement what they have learned.

The Hoback that runs through the ranch is home to the Snake River cutthroats, and you can easily wade for these fish from the banks literally right out your cabin's back door. The fish generally average fourteen to sixteen inches in length. In fact, within thirty minutes of my arrival, Dave and I were fly fishing.

Guided drift boat trips are offered on the Green River and the Snake River. Back-country horseback trips head into the wilderness, overnight if you choose. Here you will fish Willow Creek, where the fish are a bit smaller, but feed practically dawn to dusk.

The ranch's back-country camp, Hunter Creek, offers another opportunity to match wits with the wily native trout. They challenge even the most veteran fly fisherman, and present the chance for the novice to hone his skills. They maintain a policy of catch-and-release in all these waters.

Other areas where fish are plentiful include the Upper Green River. Browns, rainbows and cuts all abound here, and there is a good chance to land trophies. It is regarded as one of the West's premier trout rivers.

Still another fishery is Flat Creek, which meanders through the National Elk Refuge. The upper branch is good for experienced anglers and commonly gives up trophy-sized trout, while the lower branch is great for the beginner.

the facilities

The Spotted Horse Ranch abuts a 150,000-acre roadless area at the south end of Jackson Hole. The valley is surrounded by mountains, including the Tetons, the steepest range in North America. High mountain lakes and trails make for a perfect getaway or high country fishing adventure.

Ten cabins, all convenient to the ranch and river, house the guests. Each individual cabin, constructed of logs taken right from the surrounding forests, is quaint, rustic and full of first class appointments. The bathrooms are natural slate, and have been beautifully refurbished in keeping with the theme of casual elegance. The hot tub and sauna overlook the Hoback River, and more than forty horses are in the stable ready for riding and overnight camping trips up into the mountains.

The main lodge consists of a spacious living room with a rock fireplace. It is an open and airy place, with rafters and ceilings revealing the logs used to build it. There is definitely a "western" feel in the air, right down to the rawhide-upholstered furnishings and the coffee table, that upon closer inspection, reveals itself to be the cross section of a massive stump.

The Trout School is a great way to be introduced to Rocky Mountain trout fishing. It is a must for the new fisherman. One nod to progress is their spring-fed pond, with its own stocked cutthroat population. This is a good place for you to build confidence in the early stages of your visit.

Life at the Spotted Horse is a dramatic departure from the way most people spend their day. The pace is leisurely. You are invited to chat with the ranch hands and even take part in the ranch chores, if you wish. While a dozen of us spent most of our time fishing, others opted for a horseback ride, a float trip, a hike or an overnight camping adventure.

leisure pursuits

The town of Jackson Hole attracts visitors from around the world with legendary skiing and winterland adventures, plus thousands of acres to backpack and hike in any season. The two National Parks within close proximity, Grand Teton and Yellowstone, attract millions of visitors every year to take in the kaleidoscope of natural wonders, including the famous geysers.

Come fall, the ranch becomes headquarters for hunting trips into the Bridger-Teton National Forest. There are also two wilderness camps for hunters on the lookout for deer, moose and elk. Most of these hunts take place from the Hunter Creek Camp, sixteen miles into the back-country, at an elevation of 6,844 feet. It is the largest, and is better suited for extended stays. Martin Basin Camp is smaller and closer to the lodge. At an elevation of over 8,000 feet, it sits

in the heart of the high country on the western edge of the Greyback Ridge. Capacity is six guests at a time, and it is the more rustic of the two. Accommodations are exclusively in tents, including a heated shower tent and a cooking/dining tent.

The Spotted Horse Back-country Program allows you to become part of history as they take part in the ultimate form of travel. This popular pastime is run by Kevin Watkins. He offers a wealth of experience, with over fifteen years as a guide, packer and fly fishing buff. Witness the art of horse packing, first practiced thousands of years ago by the likes of Gengis Khan, and later by Jim Bridger and countless other mountain men as they explored and trapped the mountainous West.

the cuisine

At this resort, they employ not one, but three chefs to please your palate. Kevin Pusey and Koleen Marflak are executive chefs; Justin Raines is the sous chef. All have been trained at culinary institutes that are members of the "cordon bleu" group of schools. The focus is "ranch country" cooking, but a gourmet touch is found in many a meal, salad and dessert. The homemade ranch cookies are ever popular, and beer and wine are served in the old saloon.

Home cooked meals are served family-style in the dining room overlooking the river. Three meals are prepared each day, and their motto is simple, "quality and quantity." Also, with a little advance notice, they can cater to those guests who require a special diet.

A popular weekly event here is the steak cook-out night, right on the banks of the Hoback. It features campfire songs and a fire folks gather around, down by the river.

The evening I was there, the chefs prepared us a fabulous meal. We began with a selection of hot and cold appetizers, then went on to the main course. This was a pork tenderloin with bourbon glaze, chive whipped potatoes, and asparagus. For those who were able, a fresh homemade cheesecake was presented.

a day in the life of...clarence and rosa lee eidt

Awakening to the wonderful sounds of silence, Rosa Lee and Clarence stroll from their cabin to the main lodge for breakfast. It is just after 8:00 am. After picking up a pack lunch from the kitchen, they journey over to Star Valley to fish the spring creek there. These clear, cool waters are home to cutthroat, rainbow and brown trout.

Arriving back at the lodge at 6:00 pm, they freshen up in their cabin and join the other guests for happy hour and dinner. Tonight baked ham with sweet potatoes is on the menu. Afterwards, they relax awhile in the lounge and discuss the next day's activities. These include a trip up to Yellowstone to the Firehole River. Here, among the many active geysers, they will spend their day once again fishing for native trout.

guest comments

"I couldn't have had a better time. The food was great and staff was awesome. Thanks for making it such a memorable experience. I can't wait to return next year."

— *Brian Frost, October 2001*

" It was the best vacation our family has ever taken. Thanks for a great week."

— *Dan Hughes, July, 2002*

"Everything was Superb!!"

— *Bettina and Mark Willugn, July, 2001*

directions

The ranch sits just a few miles south and east of Jackson, Wyoming on State Highway 191. For a map and details, simply visit their website at — www.spottedhorseranch.com.

THREE RIVERS RANCH

the place

An hour north of Idaho Falls, in the foothills south of Yellowstone National Park sits the Orvis 2000 "Lodge of the Year," the Three Rivers Ranch.

Located at the confluence of Henry's Fork of the Snake River, Warm River and Robinson Creek, and bordering the Targhee National Forest, Three Rivers is a family-run operation. It has been in Lonnie's family since her grandparents, Fred and Berta Lewies, homesteaded the land in the early 1900's. The ranch grew into the Warm River Resort as it sits on what used to be a main road to Yellowstone National Park. The resort had it all — cafe, dance hall, cabins and a train stop for tourists headed to the park. Through the years it grew to encompass 700 acres.

Highway 20 changed all that, as traffic was diverted away from Warm River. Then a decision was made, and in 1974 the name was changed to Three Rivers Ranch and they began catering to fly fishing enthusiasts from all over the country. It became one of the first lodges endorsed by Orvis.

Lonnie's parents, Harry and Lillian Lewies, owned and operated the lodge, along with Lonnie's sister Julie. In 1987, Lonnie decided to buy it outright and turned it into what it is today — one of the premier fly fishing destinations in North America. Testament to this was a recent review in *Andrew Harper's Hideaway Report* that named Three Rivers Ranch one of the "Top ten fishing lodges in America."

Of even greater importance to sportsmen is the location. It is prime trout country. This resort is uniquely positioned at the heart of the west's most enjoyable and most challenging fly fishing, with easy access to Robinson Creek, Fall River, Teton River, Henry's Fork, Warm River and the South Fork of the Snake River. As their business card says, "For the discriminating fly-fisher."

the people

The people who make this place so special are actually a family. And they are now into the fourth generation. During my first day, I actually spent time with all four of them — Lonnie, her father and mother, Harry and Lillian Lewies, and her son Mitch.

The three ingredients necessary for a successful operation are good lodgings, great food and fantastic fishing. Three key people, through years of experience, have combined their talents to meet this challenge. Lonnie, as owner and manager for over fifteen years, keeps all things running smoothly. Karen Roberts, head chef for eighteen years, keeps appetites sated through creative cooking. And Doug Gibson, with thirty years as fishing guide, keeps the guests happy (with the help of his crew) by taking them to the best fishing spots.

The seventy-eight percent repeat guest rate is living proof of their success as a team.

the fishing

I arrived at Three Rivers Ranch on a morning in mid-June. In less than an hour I was settled into my cabin and introduced to Lonnie and the fishing guide staff. A good benchmark used to judge the quality of a place and its fishing is the length of time their key employees have been with them. Of their fourteen guides, three of them — Doug Gibson (head guide), Ron Heck and Paul Beckley — have been working here from twenty to thirty years each. Unheard of in this business.

Most guests seem to split their time between wading and floating these rivers. Guides coordinate weekly schedules so you can cover the most productive stretches where the hatches and conditions are currently best. Because of the variety of fishable water, fly fishing can go on from May through October uninterrupted. The guides here know these waters intimately, and precisely how to fish them. They are also known to be sensitive to the different levels of fishermen, particularly the beginner.

The season opens during the last week of May when Henry's Fork is in the middle of its Salmonfly hatch. Some real monsters can be lured to the surface by mimicking this huge stonefly. As water temperature levels off, more flies begin to emerge, and on June 15th, the famous Railroad Ranch opens, where you can experience some of the best dry fly fishing on Henry's Fork. By the end of June, the runoff is receding, and the smaller rivers are starting their runs.

July is the time of the Salmonfly hatch on the South Fork, followed by other stoneflies and mayflies. Large dries work especially well. Smaller rivers like the Teton, Fall, Robinson and Warm are running at this point, and fish extremely well. July 15th marks the opening of the Yellowstone River in Yellowstone National Park.

the facilities

Guests stay in one of seven log cabins under tall shade trees along Robinson Creek (a fine trout stream in its own right), or at Robinson Lodge. All Cabins have porches with a view of the river and forest, are furnished with antiques, are fully carpeted and have comfortable beds and electric heat. Each cabin has a private bath, and there is ample storage for all clothing and gear. They have thought of everything, right down to the covered personal rod racks. The staff and guides make your comfort and enjoyment their top priority, and it shows in the meticulous attention to detail.

The Main Lodge bar of polished mahogany and weathered logs is a natural for socializing. Wideboard floors, Oriental rugs and leather furniture all tied together nicely by an immense coffee table create the perfect story-telling atmosphere.

The Ranch is licensed to guide on an honor roll of rivers in Idaho and Montana, including the Madison, the Yellowstone, and Henry's Fork and South Fork of the Snake River. Fifteen different float trips are available. They also have an outpost camp on the South Fork which has become extremely popular with the avid fly fisherman. Capacity is eight guests.

As an Orvis-endorsed lodge, they carry only the finest in fishing gear and flies. Their guides will sit down with you before the fishing begins and decide exactly what you want to do. The guide will then devise a strategy to maximize your fishing success.

the cuisine

To fortify you for the day ahead, breakfast is always hearty. Flapjacks with syrup, sausage, eggs, bacon, ham and breads with tasty jams and jellies. Lunch is served on shore, when you are taking a break from the action.

Dining in the old lodge is an experience not to be missed. Meals are served on fine china, and good wines are poured freely into crystal goblets. The dining schedules are flexible to accommodate fishing times. You even have the option of dining well after dark. This comes as welcome news to those who would fish evening rises, or would like to float against the backdrop of an Idaho sunset.

I got lucky, arriving on a Thursday, the evening of their weekly "cook-out." We all gathered on the huge redwood deck built on the banks of the river. At 7:00 o'clock cocktails and appetizers were served. Then around 8:00 pm we all sat down and the feasting began. Dinner, of course, was a barbecue. The main course featured New Zealand Red Stag and baby back ribs, served with a huge pot of bacon and beans, a Caesar salad and garlic bread. Dessert was a chocolate mocha cheesecake.

"Wonderful fishing was available – the Teton River should not be missed. We had a 21" cutthroat, a 25" rainbow and a 17" cutthroat on successive casts in one pool of the Teton. All wading and on a dry fly!"

— *Mrs. C. R., London, England*

"Three Rivers Ranch is the first lodge we have visited offering such a variety of waters within such a short drive. What a treat to have the opportunity of fishing the Snake, Henry's Fork, Teton and Fall River or walk outside the cabin to Robinson Creek. Lonnie Allen was a fun, caring hostess who catered to our every whim."

— *Mr. & Mrs. D. C., Knoxville, Tennessee*

"My sons and I had a memorable and very pleasurable experience. We thoroughly enjoyed the accommodations, food and people. The fishing is also a great experience. The guides are people with whom you can talk and enjoy the day of fishing. Lonnie is an exceptional hostess — love your place!"

— *Mr. H. C., Somerset, Pennsylvania*

directions

Guests usually fly to Idaho Falls, Idaho. Delta has regular service from Salt Lake City, Utah. Ranch staff will meet you at the airport and drive you to the ranch. For more information, visit their website at — www.threeriversranch.com.

WEST COAST FISHING CLUB

the place

The key word in real estate, one that is also held dear in fishing resorts, is "location, location, location." The West Coast Fishing Club, situated on the Queen Charlotte Islands (also known as Haida Gwaii), has virtually cornered the market on location. As a matter of fact, they have three from which to choose. Two of the lodges, The Clubhouse and The North Island Lodge, sit on the northwest corner of the Islands. The third facility, the Outpost, is hidden in a remote rain forest twenty-six miles to the south. What makes the area so special is that virtually all major runs of salmon on the west coast of North America must pass this way on their migration routes home to their native rivers to spawn. Simply put, these places are the first sports fishing lodges to encounter the annual migration of salmon.

The Clubhouse is their premier property. It has been carved out of the forest a full 220 feet above the ocean. Upon arriving by helicopter and disembarking to the front of the lodge, you will come upon an amazing sight. You will be looking down at countless bald eagles soaring through the trees. Beyond them is a spectacular vista of ocean and forested islands.

The North Island Lodge is a floating lodge that lies in the protected side of Langara Island. The lodge is literally on the water, and the dock is actually at your doorstep. You are, therefore, literally minutes away from your next fishing adventure.

The Outpost is tucked into the rain forests and mountains streams of Graham's Island. Although only a short flight from Langara, it is located in a proposed ecological preserve. This guarantees that it will remain a true wilderness retreat forever.

Clubhouse

In order to separate themselves from the crowd, the Club has successfully created a "service culture" that is now second nature with their employees at all three operations. They have a Mission Statement that reinforces their perpetual goal of excellence. It reads:

"The West Coast Fishing Club is dedicated to offering a world class fishing experience to all members with unsurpassed levels of quality and service, which will be provided by our highly motivated and professional staff, while recognizing our responsibility to the local community and the urgent need to maintain our wilderness resources for future generations."

The Clubhouse

the people

Rick Grange and Brian Legge have been partners and friends for over three decades. Together, they built a very successful corporate security business. In fact, at the time it was sold, they employed more than 2,800 people.

Each year, they would take a number of their best clients and go salmon fishing. Blocks of rooms and boats would be booked at various fishing lodges along the Canadian west coast and the groups would arrive for some serious fishing and fun. This yearly sojourn became so popular that one year they had sixty guests descending on the Langara area at one time.

Thus the West Coast Fishing Club was born. Many of their guests wanted more - to fish in supreme style and comfort. And so it was that Rick and Brian decided to take things to the next level, and build a fishing resort without equal in North America.

The Outpost

What was initially a "fishing club", the West Coast Fishing Club has evolved into a first-class destination resort, with three separate properties, offering all the luxuries and comforts of a five-star hotel. And, of course, the best salmon fishing in the world.

The Clubhouse is run by their general manager, Robert Penman. To achieve the level of service needed in a place of this caliber, Robert oversees forty people, which is one staff member for every guest. Following his culinary training at Grosvenor House in England, he moved to Canada in 1973. His credentials include five years as Executive Chef for the Paradise Island Resort and Casino. In 1995, when visiting British Columbia, Robert met Rick and Brian and the rest, as they say, is history. He has been here since the beginning.

Before opening their new Outpost lodge in 1999, Rick and Brian were looking for someone with the right qualifications and experience in the area. They found Lisa Winbourne. A few years earlier, she had worked for a lodge on Hippa Island, just down the coast from the Outpost. Subsequent to that, she managed lodges at key fishing locales along the British Columbia coast. Glad to be "home" to the Charlottes, she opened the lodge and has been managing it ever since.

North Island Lodge stands apart from the other two properties by being the "original" West Coast Fishing Club venue and the only non-land based lodge of the three. Don Robertson has been the general manager there since 1999 when he came on board after twenty years as a fishing guide and director of fishing operations at another luxury B.C. fishing resort.

The Clubhouse

the fishing

Given their location, their claim that they offer "the best salmon fishing in the world" holds water. On our first day out, everyone caught fish. I pulled in three, although at fifteen, eighteen and twenty pounds, they were relatively small. The largest salmon of the day weighed in at fifty-two pounds. As a group, we caught a total of forty fish weighing close to a thousand pounds. Your access to all the major runs of salmon that are returning to their river systems virtually guarantees that you will have a successful fishing trip each time you head out in one of their Boston Whalers. Between strikes, take some time, as we did, to enjoy the wildlife, from the humpback whales to the massive sea lions lazing on the rocks.

The Clubhouse

While the West Coast Fishing Club provides a world-class fishing experience for all who come here, they recognize their responsibility to maintain this valuable fishing resource. To this end, guests who declare themselves "Catch and Release" will receive a gift box of wild Chinook salmon. For those who catch and release fish of forty pounds plus, they offer a selection of wonderful gifts, from Limited Edition prints to a unique piece of aquatic art by champion carver, Team Lim. For the over-fifty release crowd, the choice is a tough one — an MR2 Islander Precision Reel valued at over $550 or a custom commissioned replica fiberglass mount of your fish.

In the last several years, due to diligent management, levels of Chinook and Coho salmon have returned to numbers not seen in years. Guests in late season (August and September) are reporting catching more than thirty fish each day. The size and numbers of fish have been steadily climbing year after year. In the summer of 2000, after an exhausting ninety minute battle, one of their guests landed a record halibut — a 325 pound behemoth.

The Outpost

The Clubhouse

The phenomenal fishing at the Outpost is consistent for one reason. The water depth drops sharply, creating deep holes that hold bait and keep salmon in the feeding grounds for long periods of time. For those who want to fish truly "unfished waters", a heli-lift from the Outpost will fly fishermen to virgin rivers and lakes to fish for Dolly Varden and Cutthroat trout.

the facilities

The Clubhouse is the ultimate in luxury. It is spacious, spanning an incredible 22,000 square feet. This does not include its 10,000-square-foot deck. The post-and-beam structure has been built to blend in with the natural woodland surroundings. There is a huge fireplace in the common area, along with a bar, satellite television, pool table and library. They even have an upper lounge complete with shuffleboard, piano and the latest first-run movies. It is tastefully appointed throughout, with rare original artwork adorning most walls, and a private dining room that features seventeenth-century antique sterling silverware. The solarium dining room makes every meal an event, with its wilderness vistas. All accommodations are under one roof. They have nineteen rooms that will handle up to thirty-six guests. All rooms have en suite facilities, and ten have views overlooking the ocean.

This lodge also has the facilities to accommodate business meetings. For those groups, they provide the upper lounge and use of the private dining room. It has become quite popular with the "white collar crowd" as a corporate retreat. Capacity is sixteen people.

The Outpost

To maximize your fishing adventures, the West Coast Fishing Club's fleet of seventeen- and nineteen-foot Boston Whalers is more than adequate. They also have an offshore fleet that enables you to go where most can't. These boats range from twenty-two to twenty-seven feet and come fully equipped. Features on board include VHF radios, depth finders, compasses, survival suits and all necessary tackle. The biggest boats also have GPS, electric downriggers, and halibut and shark gear.

The Clubhouse — Upper Lounge

The North Island Lodge might look ordinary from the outside, but it is pure posh on the inside. It is anchored in Beal Cove, just a stone's throw from the Clubhouse. Comfortably housing twenty-four guests at a time, their spacious rooms all have en suite washrooms. Quite a luxury for a floating lodge. They feature a large lounge with wet bar and fireplace, a dining room, and even a games area. While they are well known for the fishing, the food here has gained quite a reputation in recent years. Chef Walter and his staff seem to be the secret ingredient.

The fleet employed in this location includes nineteen- and twenty-one-foot Eaglecraft aluminum boats. All enjoy the same features as the Clubhouse vessels. Because of the area, guests are fitted with all-weather ocean suits.

In their continuing effort to provide the absolute best in deluxe fishing vacations, Rick and Brian have put plans in motion to take the North Island Lodge to new heights. Scheduled to open within two years, the new facility will be the best luxury floating lodge in North America. The timber frame construction will use hand-peeled, twelve-by-twelve beams. It will reach 170 feet in length and rise three stories high. The total finished area will be over 20,000 square feet. There will, of course, be first-class amenities throughout including two hot tubs, two lounges, a main dining room, a private dining room, a sauna, steam room, an exercise area and massage therapy.

Their newest facility is the Outpost. Situated on one of the two largest islands in the Queen Charlotte chain, this lodge is just a brief helicopter ride from the Clubhouse. It sits secluded in the rain forest on

The Clubhouse

Riddall Cove, the island's most natural harbor, in a pristine wilderness. As expected, I found the Outpost to be spacious, comfortable and richly appointed. The lodge has been designed and built to reflect the wilderness it sits in. The main lodge features eight rooms, two luxury suites with fireplaces, balconies and en suite Jacuzzi tubs. The main lounge was built with comfort in mind — overstuffed chairs, large fireplace, pool table, wet bar and even satellite communications, if needed.

The Clubhouse Suite

leisure pursuits

After a long day on the water, the Clubhouse has a variety of exercise equipment for both fitness and relaxation. The Spa features treadmills and stationary bicycles, as well as a steam room, sauna and a hot tub overlooking Parry Passage. They even have a resident Massage Therapist.

The three locations offer a treasure trove of non-fishing activities. Throughout the season, guests can do some serious whale watching, sometimes up-close and personal when they come within a few feet of the boat. Schools of porpoise regularly buzz the island, keeping pace with even the fastest outboard boats. Langara is also a haven for bird watchers, and sighting a Peregrine falcon, albatross, puffin or Bald eagle is a common experience. Down at the Outpost, guests simply relax in this unique natural setting. Deer, elk and bear freely roam this sanctuary.

For those guests who like to stay active and outdoors, the resort offers sea kayaking and hiking through old-growth forests. For the ultimate outdoor experience, some guests take the "Heli-Hike." Along with a native guide, they are airlifted to a mountain peak where the challenge is to make it home. Those who have done this say there is nothing with which to compare it.

The Clubhouse

the cuisine

The Clubhouse's solarium dining room is in a class all by itself. Stepping down into the main salon, you are greeted by the most magnificent panorama — ocean, sky, eagles and forest. This is where everyone meets for the three meals prepared each day. At each meal, they offer a

The Clubhouse

full selection of entrées to accommodate the multitude of tastes or dietary requirements of all guests. Rather than singing the praises of their cuisine, I will simply list what was on the menu during my second day.

For breakfast, which is served from 6:30 am to 9:30 am, guests chose from a selection that included Eggs Benedict, Eggs Florentine, Huevos Rancheros and Strawberry Pancakes. The chef will also gladly prepare anything you ask for.

For those of us who made it back for lunch, the offerings included Ribeye Steak with green peppercorn au jus and herb-crusted halibut with tomato confit. During lunch, you are asked to view the dinner menu and make your selections for the evening.

Dinner, of course, is the main event. Around 7:00 pm, after the day's fishing, all guests converge in the living room where happy hour and hors d'oeuvres are in full swing. Then at 8:00 pm you are called to the dining room.

Our three-course meal began with Truffle cauliflower soup, with Stilton creme brulee. This was followed by the main course — cinnamon smoked duck breast, served with roasted pear and talegio ravioli, and ver jus brown butter. Dessert finished our meal — a champagne and passion fruit parfait.

The Clubhouse

a day in the life of…patrick loubert

As if often the case, Patrick heard about this place from friends in his hometown, Toronto, Ontario. When I met him, he was enjoying his third consecutive year here. He wakes just after 5:30 am. After a quick shower, it's off to the dining room for breakfast and discussions with his partners on what may be the best fishing spots for the day. Then they head down to the dock, meet with their guide, and are on the water by 7:15 am.

Patrick will usually fish a full day - ten to twelve hours. If he's landed a few salmon in the morning hours, then lunch back at the lodge is in order. But if the fishing is lean, he will stay out on the water for the day. Lunch then involves flagging down the lodge's courtesy boat, which will meet up with them and deliver sandwiches, snacks and drinks.

He will usually arrive back at the lodge by 7:00 pm. After freshening up in his room, he will join the group for cocktails, hors d'oeuvres and dinner. Bedtime is usually around 10:00 pm.

guest comments

"What an extraordinary place, staff and facilities. I will never forget the opportunity of watching my son land an 18-pound Coho and join the Tyee Club with a 31-pound King!"

— *Actor Peter Coyote, Mill Valley, California*

"As good as it gets — any better, never leave."

— *Broadcaster Keith Jackson, Sherman Oaks, California*

"A five-star Lodge, no exceptions. The very best in my 20 years of fishing Canadian waters."

— *Bob Alessandro, Gig Harbor, Washington*

"You are the Pebble Beach of great fishing."

— *John Baumann, Cincinnati, Ohio*

"I have waited 72 years for this!

— *Len Graves, Dartmouth, Nova Scotia*

"Sets a new standard for fishing lodges."

— *Phillip Bond, West Vancouver, B.C.*

directions

Located in the beautiful Queen Charlotte Islands, the West Coast Fishing Club resorts are easily accessible through Vancouver International Airport in Canada. Once you arrive, they will arrange a flight on one of their corporate planes up to Masset, B.C. The airport also has the facilities to handle corporate jets and, for direct flights in from the U.S., they can clear customs. From there, they will helicopter you to your chosen destination. For more information, visit their website at — www.westcoastfishingclub.com.

The Clubhouse

WIT'S END GUEST RANCH

the place

If sitting behind a desk for fifty hours a week has you at your wit's end, then that might be just the prescription. Wit's End, that is. The Wit's End Guest Ranch in southwestern Colorado.

They'll tell you that nothing major has happened here, except a lot of kids and horses raised, lots of fish caught, along with a tradition of hospitality spanning close to 150 years. Then, in the same breath, they will tell you of the Dalton Gang, Teddy Roosevelt, and of the golden treasures in the lost mines up in "them thar hills."

The ranch was founded by the Patrick family in 1859. By the late 1880's, the ranch had grown, had pooled the waters from creeks feeding the lake and had established a hatchery for the native trout. It is a fishing infrastructure that pays dividends yet today.

In its present incarnation, the Wit's End Guest Ranch is the brainchild of Jim Custer, and is a fishing paradise. It sits in the breathtaking Vallecito Lake Valley, nestled between 12,000- and 14000-foot granite peaks and an aspen and pine forest. Known worldwide for its outstanding fly fishing, this resort is an Orvis-endorsed fishing lodge. It is also exceptionally family-friendly, and has summer children's and teens' programs.

Guests have access to both high-country and low-country excursions. The high-country trips are designed to take advantage of the deep mountain lakes in the area. Low-country trips will take you to several rivers, including the San Juan and Animas. Both these waters are rated in the Top 100 in the country by *Trout Unlimited,* and offer the potential of hooking a true trophy.

the people

Within thirty minutes of my arrival, I had met no less than ten of the ranch staff. To a person, they were relaxed, friendly and well-informed. Jack Denton is the head wrangler. A true cowboy, he has won two world championships for roping. Their fly-fishing program is run by Mike Paterniti, who has been a certified casting instructor for twenty years.

The owner of this resort, Jim Custer, has an interesting background. Back in the early 1960's he began a career in real estate development. Twenty-five years later his own real estate company, specializing in apartment building sales, owned almost 3,000 units. In 2000, after thirty-five years in the business, Jim decided to slow down and sold off most of his properties.

During these successful years, another opportunity presented itself in the form of an aerospace company. Space Data was a prime contractor building and testing sub-orbital rocket ships. Under Jim's and his partners' watch, the company grew from eighty to 300 people. In 1988, after merging with Orbital Sciences, they went public. The new company manufactured and flew the first commercially feasible rocket ship capable of orbiting satellites. They also launched a Mars fly-by mission.

In 1986, a property near his second home in the Vallecito Lake Valley came up for sale. It was the Wit's End Ranch. Closed down since the mid-1970's, Jim bought and rehabilitated the old cabins and ancient barn. Two years later he had created a world class guest ranch. Eleven years after opening, Wit's End Guest Ranch proudly became the forty-second fly fishing lodge in North America to be endorsed by Orvis. High praise indeed.

the fishing

Fly fishing is what it's all about here, be it in lake or fast-flowing river (how fast is decided by the previous winter's snowfall). A few hours of fishing around the Ranch is a great way to shake off the rust or learn the ropes before trekking out on a longer excursion. Three stocked ponds and a two-day comprehensive introduction are available for those who are just starting out. Their expert instructors have been teaching techniques and strategies for years, and teach to the level of the angler. Within one hour they can put you on seven different rivers and three different lakes.

For the more experienced and adventurous, over twenty lakes await in the high country, including Colorado's largest natural one, Emerald Lake. Trout in this lake average sixteen inches, with plenty in the twenty-plus range. Other prime fishing areas include the Pine, Vallecito and Florida Rivers. The Pine is a great brown trout producer, but also has a good population of rainbow and cutthroat. The Vallecito and Florida have a few browns, but are better known for their rainbow, cutthroat, and brookies.

All these trips are via horseback, with a wrangler and a fly fishing guide along for the ride. Minimum duration is three days, so you'll be sleeping under the stars and eating freshly prepared "campfire" meals, while you fish these incredible waters.

In some circles, the San Juan River is considered to be one of the three best trout fishing rivers in the United States. Rainbows here average three to five pounds, and there are plenty of them. Hook one of these on a size 20 midge, and at the end of the day your aching wrists will remind you that you're having the time of your life.

the facilities

Accommodations at Wit's End Ranch are, to say the least, first class. They have received four stars from the Star Rating Service. *Country Inns* magazine rated it "one of the twelve best in America," and *Reed's Official Hotel Guide* calls it, "One of the best three dude ranches in America." Their theme is rustic opulence at the edge of the wilderness.

The resort, sitting on 550 acres at an elevation of over 7,800 feet, offers two separate properties. The original Wit's End is at one end, the Orvis-endorsed Streamside Lodge is at the other. During peak season, their staff of sixty-five will look after a capacity of 130 guests.

These guests stay in one- to four-bedroom log cabins scattered around the properties. They are strategically placed to afford the greatest possible view of the countryside. And all cabins are wonderfully appointed, with queen-sized beds, down comforters, stone fireplaces, full kitchens with country china, Berber carpets and even porch swings.

The centerpiece of the ranch, nicknamed the "Old Lodge at the Lake," is originally the old barn that John Patrick built back in 1870. This grand structure is the center of activity.

Wit's End Guest Ranch

leisure pursuits

While I enjoyed the fishing here, horseback riding was also popular with the crowd. A stable of close to 120 horses will help you explore the almost one million acres of the San Juan National Forest. Whether trail riding or mountain riding, the choice is left up to each visitor.

For those in the mood, they even offer a complete spa facility. There are massage therapy rooms, a swedish sauna, a steam shower, and two hot tubs. If you are feeling adventurous, ask about their "hot rocks" therapy massage.

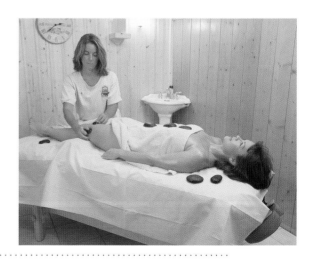

Historic Durango is nearby, and guests can trek over there to enjoy the local offerings, including the Durango-Silverton Narrow Gauge Train, whitewater rafting, golf, skiing the Ute Mountains, and the Mesa Verda Indian ruins.

the cuisine

All meals are prepared and served in the "Old Lodge." Every morning begins with a fresh pot of coffee, warm muffins, buttermilk biscuits, and a fresh fruit plate. Then it's time for breakfast.

Depending on the mood of the chef, the dinner menu can range from a classic French to Western Barbecue. A sample of the fare might include smoked beef brisket (cooked on a spit in the open flame), grilled trout, walleye, and baked beans, potato salad, coleslaw, corn bread. Dessert might be homemade peach cobbler with ice cream.

They also take their fine dining very seriously. For this they turn to Master Chef Peter Holder. His wealth of experience includes executive chef at the Ritz in London, six years at the famous Charlie's Crab in Palm Beach, and three years with the Royal Family as their Maitre de Cuisine.

A sampling of his gourmet fare might include baked brie Encrute, sundried tomato leek soup, baby spinach with hot bacon vinaigrette, and pan fried chicken with artichoke hearts. Desserts on the "gourmet" side include poached pear in a praline basket and wildberry coulet.

guest comments

"For the past 25 years, our family has enjoyed vacations and adventures on both coasts and at international resorts. Wit's End is extra ordinary, surpassing all the rest. We look forward to many future visits. Thank you again for sharing your treasure, Wit's End, with all of us."

— *John and Carolyn Newman, Rye, New York*

"My families' stay at Wit's End…was truly one of the best vacations my family has taken and this can be attributed to the fine staff and management you have on the property not to mention the many amenities and exceptional ranch you maintain. We parted from your ranch with fond memories that will last us a lifetime."

— *Carl Ruderman, New York, New York*

"Once again, we want to say thanks for a wonderful week. What a breath of fresh air! We will always be grateful and remember you always."

— *Rick and Mary Underwood, Richmond, Virginia*

"Out of this world! A pleasant surprise — better than anticipated. There was not anyone that would not go out of their way to accommodate and serve us. You truly have a fun, hardworking staff there. Thanks for a fantastic week."

— *Bud and Dee Grell, Louisville, Kentucky*

directions

Most visitors to this guest ranch will fly into Durango, Colorado. Wit's End is located just 24 miles northeast, directly off County Road 500 and Highway 160 in Vallecito Lake. For more information, see their website at — www.witsendranch.com.

WOOD RIVER LODGE

the place

Set in the shadow of rugged Jackknife Mountain and Bumyok Ridge is the Wood River Lodge. Located within the 1,500,000-acre Wood Tikchik State Park in western Alaska, mountains, rivers, glaciers and wildlife are at your beck and call. In this park you will find grizzly bear (brown bear), black bear, moose, wolf and caribou, as well as numerous birds including the bald and golden eagle, tundra swan and waterfowl. And, of course, some of the finest fishing in the world.

The scenery has to be seen to be believed. This area carries the scars of its glacial past like badges of honor, with the perpetrators still loitering to take in their handiwork. Lakes up to sixty miles long dot the landscape. Glaciers hanging over lakes, and snow-covered peaks provide opportunities for the photographs of a lifetime.

River Bay on the Agulowak River was once a native campsite, used by the locals to accumulate winter stores of fish and game. Centuries later in the 1940's, white settlers homesteaded about thirty acres, the descendants of whom still live in the area. In the 1960's, the property was sold to a fishing guide who built what would become the main lodge of what is now the Wood River Lodge.

The resort sits on the banks of the Agulowak River, a river so plentiful in trout that the Alaska Department of Fish and Wildlife has designated it the most productive rainbow water in the state. The count is an amazing 4,000 rainbow trout per mile of river. The fishing here is so good that the lodge's return/referral guest rate is usually around eighty percent. So I wasn't really surprised to count seven fish jumping near the shore as we came in for a landing; and twenty minutes later, to hear a guest tell us of the twenty-six inch rainbow he caught on his first cast.

the people

In the early 1980's, a group from Fairbanks, Alaska bought the property and built some guest cabins. It was first run as the Wood River Lodge in 1983. In 1987, Bernie Ortman was hired as a pilot and guide. A year later, his father, John Ortman, came on as a pilot and guide as well. That year, Wood River Lodge was named "Alaska Lodge of the Year." Over the years more of the Ortman family joined the staff. Bernie's oldest son Jacob started in 1990, at the age of eleven, washing dishes and cleaning fish. Now, following in his father's footsteps, he is one of the lodge's pilots and guides.

Wood River Lodge is totally family owned and operated. Most of their staff has been with them for years. They understand that the primary goal of each and every one of them is to see that their guests have an experience of a lifetime. Their staff-to-guest ratio is one-to-one. Their guides are all fully licensed, and have been trained in CPR and First Aid. They know the waters they fish and how to fish them. They teach fly tying, fly casting and spin casting. When it comes to local fishing knowledge, their guides are considered by many to be the best in the state of Alaska.

the fishing

The fishing from Wood River Lodge is in a class of its own. The Bristol Bay salmon runs are world-renowned. You will fish the rivers, streams and lakes that are the spawning grounds for this famous fishery. During king/chinook salmon season it is not unusual to catch ten to twenty salmon a day, some weighing up to sixty-five pounds. The kings run from mid-June through the end of July. The Sockeye, or Red salmon, always a challenge to catch, swim just thirty feet from your cabin door. Their run begins in late June and continues through August. Typically 1.5 million sockeye salmon will enter the Wood River, the majority of which will pass right in front of the lodge. Late June or early July is the best time to catch them on a well-presented fly

or lure. About the end of July they have begun to turn color and have developed the green head and hooked nose that they are so famous for.

The coho, or silver salmon runs begin the first of August and continue through the end of the season. To catch a fifteen-pound silver salmon on a seven-weight rod is an experience you will never forget. You just pray your line won't break while your sparring partner is jumping, leaping, dancing on its tail and running.

Two other salmon varieties found here are pinks and chum. Wood River Lodge is strategically located so that many of the lakes and rivers can be reached without the use of an aircraft. Because of this, you are able to fish quality areas even when the weather precludes flyout fishing. This entire fishery is also available for evening fishing. Their guides are available to fish with you as late as 10:00 pm during the summer, and until thirty minutes before dark in the fall. Lake trout are also available in Wood Tikchik State Park. You can spend a day casting for huge lake trout from the shores of the Tikchik Lakes, flying from spot to spot to find just that perfect cover for shore lunch. Here you can enjoy fresh-caught lakers sizzling in the pan, with onions, potatoes and beans.

The rainbows are available all season. They get fatter and fatter as they feed on the smolt and then the eggs of the salmon. By late August and into September, the Sockeye have turned a brilliant red and are holding at the mouth of their stream, waiting for the moment to enter and spawn. After spawning, their life cycle complete, they die and the rainbow, Dolly Varden, Arctic char and grayling are all there to take part in this never ending circle of life.

the facilities

In 1992, the rebuilding and modernizing of the facilities began. By the end of the 1997 season the project was completed. That year, the Wood River Lodge was again named Alaska's "Lodge of the Year." Although modern, the resort still retains it's original rustic charm, down to the sixteen-foot long native spruce dining table and the other handmade furnishings.

The resort features four guest cabins, with accommodations for a maximum of sixteen people. Each cabin has two rooms, with two twin beds and a private bath. These cabins are comfortable and private, and just a short walk from the main lodge facility. The main lodge has a dining room, a comfortable living room with a fireplace and bar, and a small fly tying area.

The lodge has a fleet of three aircraft, two Dehaviland Beavers and an amphibious Dehaviland Otter. The capacity of these aircraft and their performance allows them to take you, your guides and equipment to any of the rivers, streams or lakes you choose to fish. The size of their fleet ensures that each guest can fly to their destination of choice; without the necessity of shuttling, and cutting seriously into your fishing time. The pilots are all professional and have thousands of hours of seaplane time.

Wood River has a fleet of twenty-five boats, most of which are positioned on lakes or rivers throughout the Bristol Bay region. These boats are equipped with jet engines, each capable of running in as little as three inches of water. They also have a complete complement of boats located at the lodge for you to enjoy evening fishing. One boat I saw was a sight to behold. A twenty-four-foot Almar that combines the ultimate in speed and power with a 460-horsepower Ford engine.

For the business client, they offer corporate retreats. Here, they rent the entire lodge for a week. You may bring a total of sixteen guests at a time, or two different groups during the week, to accommodate thirty-two guests. No non-corporate guests are present during these weeks.

the cuisine

Mornings at Wood River are special. A beverage of your choice is brought to your cabin about forty minutes before breakfast, which is served at 7:00 am. You sit down to a table laden with food. Homemade bread, eggs done the way you like them, hot cereal, bacon or sausage, hashbrowns, fresh fruit and juice. After breakfast, your guide will meet you at the plane or boat to begin your day of fishing. Your lunch will have been carefully packed, unless you choose to have a shore lunch of freshly fried fish.

Dinner on the day I was visiting began with appetizers, including a delicious halibut mousse with crackers, and a smoked salmon and cheese tray. The main meal featured a Caesar salad, Hickory-smoked, honey glazed Baked Ham, rosemary red potatoes, sauteed spring vegetables, and freshly baked sesame egg bread. Dessert was a chocolate mousse served in a chocolate cup.

a day in the life of…don marsh

Don and his son Dave have been coming to the Wood River Lodge every year for the last decade plus. Owner of Marsh Supermarkets in Indianapolis, Indiana, Don loves this place so much that, several years ago, he decided to begin bringing members of his staff as well as merchandise suppliers. The ultimate perk.

After morning coffee and juice delivered by the staff, they come down for breakfast around 7:00 o'clock. Then its down to the dock to meet up with their guide and fly out to the day's fishing adventure. After a full day on the water, including a break for shore lunch, they all return to the lodge around 5:30 pm for cocktails and conversation. A resounding ring of the bell announces dinner at 7:00 pm. Afterwards, Don and the other guests visit with the chief guide to custom plan the next day's fishing.

guest comments

"I won't soon forget the first time I fished at lovely Wood River Lodge in the Wood River/Tikchik Lakes region in southwestern Alaska. The river we were at looked for all the world like we'd died and gone to rainbow, grayling and char heaven - all in one. Fish of all sizes and species were rising to naturals all around us. It was just like I had always imagined fly fishing utopia would be - ever since I began dreaming about rainbow trout on a full time basis some years ago."

— *Dan Heiner, Author of Alaska on The Fly.*

"Wood River Lodge has access to the best fishing I have ever seen. Located 350 miles from the nearest road system, this rustic/comfortable lodge puts you minutes away from great catches of 11 different species. From this lodge you can catch all five species of Pacific salmon, arctic char, grayling, northern pike, lake trout, rainbow trout and Dolly Varden. Not only is this the best fishing I've ever experienced, it is perhaps the most beautiful setting. The Wood River-Tikchik Lake region is a spectacular wilderness park comprising two separate systems of large, interconnected pristine lakes. Rugged mountains form the backdrop for some of the lakes on the western side of the park. One the eastern side, the lakes run into arctic tundra.

— *Tom Gresham, Field Editor, Sports Afield Magazine*

directions

The major airlines fly into Anchorage. From there, you also have a variety of air carriers that service Dillingham, including Alaska Airlines, Penair and Reeve Aleution Airways. From Dillingham, you will be picked up by one of their planes and flown to the lodge. For more information check out their website at — www.woodriverlodge.com.

YES BAY LODGE

the place

Down on the very southeast tip of Alaska, about fifty miles from Ketchikan, sits Revillagigedo Island. It is separated from the mainland by the Behm Canal, a twisting circular fjord-like channel that is home to glacier-carved canyons, inlets and secluded bays. This island, measuring fifty-five miles long and thirty-five miles wide is mostly inaccessible to human traffic. One of the coves is called Yes Bay. First explored by the Tlinglet tribe, the area was given its name from their native word for the local blue mussel - yaas.

In the 1950's, the surrounding timber and commercial fishing industries were building a strong economy for the Alaskan workers. This newly affluent population was offered entertainment in the form of casinos, saloons and cat houses in and around the Ketchikan area. In 1956, an entrepreneur broke ground for a new casino and cat house on Yes Bay. Three years later, Alaska became the 49th state in the Union. Part of the bargain for statehood was the elimination of all gambling and prostitution. Thus, the new casino was never completed. This place is now the home of the Yes Bay Lodge.

the people

The lodge is owned and operated by the Hack family. The patriarch, Art Hack, after a successful career in the Navy as a pilot, moved his family to Alaska and started an air taxi company called Tyee Airlines. In 1976, his teenage sons Bill and Kevin spent their summer as guides for K & L, the owners of Yes Bay Lodge at the time. When Art and his wife Marlys visited their sons, they knew that they had found their new home. In 1977, the family bought the lodge and immediately began developing it into one of the first successful fishing lodges in southeast Alaska.

Today, Bill Hack and his family live and work full time at the lodge. Kevin, following in his father's footsteps, owns an air taxi service called Promech Air, serving outlying communities and tourists through flight-seeing tours.

the fishing

Yes Bay offers both fresh and saltwater fishing. From their dock, you can go anywhere to troll or drift mooch for salmon, or bottom jig for halibut and rockfish. The steelhead fishing in the rivers tumbling down from

the mountain slopes is fantastic, with fish averaging eight to ten pounds. The myriad lakes, streams and rivers within a short distance of the lodge offer some of the finest trout and Dolly Varden fishing in the state.

There are five species of salmon that spawn in this area, including king, sockeye, coho, pink and chum. We went fishing in one of their twenty-foot custom-built covered boats. It was equipped with state-of-the-art equipment, including depth and fish finders, downriggers and graphite rods and reels. All fishing adventures are fully guided, and the lodge limits each boat to two guests.

I decided to fish for salmon - a fish that, pound for pound, is one the fiercest fighters in the world. My prize catch of the day was a thirty-seven pound king. He ran four times during our half hour battle. We photographed and measured our fish before releasing him back into the waters. I wanted a trophy wall mount for my den.

the facilities

The lodge has been designed with style and comfort in mind. The centerpiece is their dining room, with huge picture windows offering an expansive vista of the bay and beyond. Adjacent to this is the bar and lounge area, where fishermen congregate at day's end to share their stories.

Branching out in two directions from this main area are hallways leading to the guest rooms. These are

deluxe accommodations, all with views of the surrounding bay and forest. Their capacity is only twenty-four people. With a experienced staff of thirty on board, personal service is a given.

For those anglers who feel they did not get enough exercise while out on the water, they have built an exercise room on their property. It comes complete with Soloflex, nautilus, treadmill and stationary bicycles.

The Yes Bay Lodge also features a conference room for its corporate clients. Whether it's a convention, board meeting, or sales incentive program they have the tools necessary to make it successful.

leisure pursuits

There are a wealth of activities available for all who come here. Hiking is quite popular, and you will find several nature trails through the rainforest surrounding the lodge. Be advised that these hikes are classified as moderate to very strenuous.

Another enjoyable pastime is kayaking. The lodge provides single and two-man kayaks for both the novice and expert alike. If you are new to the sport, they will introduce you to the basic maneuvers and safety tips that are common knowledge among veterans. While out paddling on these protected waters, you may experience some fantastic wildlife encounters - black or brown bear, eagles, deer, killer whales, porpoise and sea otters.

the cuisine

Breakfast begins at 7:00 am. In addition to the morning special of the day, we were offered a buffet of coffee, juices, fresh fruits, cereals and an array of homemade baked goods. You have your choice for lunch. If you come back to the lodge from your fishing adventure, they will serve you in the dining room. However, I found that most guests took a packed lunch with them for an uninterrupted day on the water.

Dinnertime is a memorable affair, and always features at least a three-course meal. The family has been collecting their favorite Alaskan recipes for more than twenty years. Many of these dishes benefit from the fresh fish and shellfish brought in daily by the local fishermen. I was fortunate enough to be there for their famous "seafood buffet" night — mouth-watering platters of fresh seafood set in an all-you-can-eat atmosphere. Selections included salmon, halibut, dungeness crab and jumbo shrimp. Our dessert that evening was Swedish cream in Grand Marnier sauce.

guest comments

"Yes Bay Lodge is the premiere lodge in southeast Alaska. For the last twenty-five years it has provided my family and friends nature at its finest, Alaskan fishing, and photography at its best. Yes Bay has always provided us with superb food and lodging in a friendly family atmosphere that can only be found with the Hack family and their talented, loyal crew of guides and staff who have returned year after year."

— *Pete Gwosdof, Anaheim, California*

"I spent eight years planning for my "once-in-a lifetime" fishing trip to Alaska. I am so thankful to the travel agent who referred me to Yes Bay Lodge near Ketchikan. After my third trip to Yes Bay Lodge in the past four years, the staff and owners have become part of my "extended" family. You just can't beat the fishing or the warm hospitality anywhere else!"

— *Russell B. Finton, Orlando, Florida*

directions

Yes Bay is located about fifty miles north of Ketchikan, off the northwestern portion of the Behm Canal. The resort is on the mainland, sitting in the Tongass National Forest. Alaska Airlines serves Ketchikan daily with regular flights from many major cities in the lower forty-eight. Upon your arrival at the airport, the lodge's pilot will meet you. From there it is only a twenty minute floatplane flight to the resort. For more information visit their website at — www.yesbay.com.

CONTACT INFORMATION

BARANOF WILDERNESS LODGE
Address: P.O. Box 2187 • Sitka, AK 99835
Telephone: (800) 613 - 6551 • Fax: (530) 582 - 8139
Email: mtrotter@flyfishalaska.com • Website: flyfishalaska.com
Photo Credits: John Hendrikson

BUFFALO CREEK RANCH
Address: P.O. Box 2 • 2320 JCR 28A • Rand, CO 80473
Telephone: (970) 723 - 8311 • Fax: (970) 723 - 4330
Email: mical@buffalocreek-ranch.com • Website: buffalocreek-ranch.com
Photo Credits: Robin Proctor

DELAWARE RIVER CLUB
Address: HC-1, Box 1290 • Starlight, PA 18461
Telephone: (800) 662 - 9359 • Fax: (570) 635 - 5844
Email: drc@panix.com • Website: mayfly.com
Photo Credits: Richard Franklin, Joe Dimaggio

FIREHOLE RANCH
Address: Box 686 • W. Yellowstone, MT 59758
Telephone: (406) 646 - 7294 • Fax: (406) 646 - 4728
Email: info@fireholeranch.com • Website: fireholeranch.com
Photo Credits: Ken Takata

FISHING UNLIMITED
Address: P.O. Box 19301 • Anchorage, AK 99519
Telephone: (907) 243 - 5899 • Fax: (907) 243 - 2473
Email: info@alaskasfishingunlimited.com • Website: alaskalodge.com
Photo Credits: Barry & Kathy Beck